Ben Ami Levavi

Garden of Secrets

All Mysteries of the Bible Revealed

A Literary and Historical Anthology

Ben Ami Levavi

Garden of Secrets

All Mysteries of the Bible Revealed

A Literary and Historical Anthology

Senior Editors & Producers: Contento
Translator: Zvi Chazanov
Editor: Sherill Layton
Design: Amit Dey
Cover Design: Liliya Lev Ari

Copyright © 2015 by Ben Ami Levavi and Contento

All rights reserved. No part of this book may be translated, reproduced, stored in a retrieval system or transmitted, in any form or by any means, electronic, photocopying, recording or otherwise, without prior permission in writing from the author and publisher.

ISBN: 978-965-550-312-8

International sole distributor: Contento
22 Isserles Street, 6701457 Tel Aviv, Israel

www.ContentoNow.com
netanel@contento-publishing.com

Ben Ami Levavi

Garden of Secrets

All Mysteries of the Bible Revealed

A Literary and Historical Anthology

TABLE OF CONTENTS

Prologue.. vii

Chapter 1: In the Beginning, God Hath Created 1

Chapter 2: Enuma Elish | Epic of Creation 8

Chapter 3: The Creation of Man.................................. 61

Chapter 4: The Nephilim Were on Earth 67

Chapter 5: The Flood | Water upon Earth......................... 77

Chapter 6: Abraham in the Service of the Gods 88

Chapter 7: Destruction upon Sumer 101

Chapter 8: Secret of the Pyramid 106

Chapter 9: The Prisoner in the Pyramid 114

Chapter 10: Yahweh is God..................................... 118

Chapter 11: Landing on Earth 126

Summary... 132

Epilogue... 137

B. A. Levavi: The Ancient World 140

Index 167

PROLOGUE

The Bible was my childhood companion. My father and teacher, may he rest in peace, was a Bible, Talmud, and Jewish Law Interpretations teacher in a Jewish Orthodox school, and thus believed I must become just as erudite as he had been. As a child, I approached the Bible with great awe and love, which bred my religious conviction as self-evident, making me regard the Lord's actions and commandments as unquestionably sacred. When I grew up, questions and doubts started to shake the foundations of my God-fearing convictions: God, being an anthropomorphic entity, "**let us make man in our image, after our likeness**" (*Genesis* 1:26), and is the Creator of the entire world with His word; He walks about the Garden, searching for Adam; the Creator of the Tree of Life and Tree of Knowledge; Serpent and Eve; the Daughters of Men, bearing children to the Sons of God, mentioned in Genesis 6; the year and ten days Noah had spent on his Ark with every beast, a male and a female of each species, and seven of each clean beast; all these stories raise plenty of questions and wonderment. Likewise, the Books of Joshua, Judges, and the rest of the Hebrew Bible are ample with dilemmas and enigmas. As kabbalists had correctly stated, the Bible is PARDES, literally meaning "garden," but also the Hebrew acronym of *pshat*, or the literal meaning; *remez*, or hint; *drash*, interpretation, and *sod*, or secret meaning; to study the Bible means to explore deeply into that garden of parabolic and allegorical expressions. Literal meaning offers hints, which one must interpret and examine in order to find the secret meaning, and figure out what the biblical verse fully means. Eventually, I reached the plausible conclusion, that, indeed, it is the Book's very early times, many thousands of years ago, with which we are dealing. Therefore, one may assume that before scripture, stories were passed through the ages albeit distorted, changed, and blended with fantasies and wishful thinking, drifting away from their original form and meaning. Thus I started thinking of searching for the origin, that is, narratives, documents and texts from the dawn of existence accurately informing us about that very beginning of time and history.

In the course of time, numerous tables, pictures, images, cylinder stamps, inscribed stones and other artifacts have been discovered, deciphered and translated, shedding additional light on the contents concealed within them for millennia, before being unearthed by archaeologists. Most of these findings originated from the royal libraries of the rulers of Nineveh, Nippur and other ancient Sumerian cities. In each of these cities, over 25,000 clay tablets have been stored, written in Mesopotamian cuneiforms. Many other documents have been discovered in other parts of the Ancient World, namely the ruins of Acadia, Land of the Hittites, Egypt and Africa. Many of them present advanced scientific knowledge in fields such as genetics, electronics, and space, knowledge discovered by mankind only as late as the second part of the 20th Century.

The recent technological progress gave mankind the means to understand many findings, which had puzzled us until recently. This also is what makes the Pentateuch so magnificent: while referring to the earliest stage of universal and Jewish history, it associates it with knowledge of the natural sciences, computers, spacecraft, telecommunication and genetic engineering, which is increasingly revealed to us with the advancement of modern science.

Cuneiform clay tablets, preserved intact until being discovered by archaeologists in Mesopotamia, are the earliest known narratives found. Telling the story of a most ancient civilization that existed on this part of the Earth, they are the most original and reliable sources of additional information on the Bible and early history of humanity and the planet Earth. The Enuma Elish story of Creation, fully presented in this book, is a most important epic discovered by archaeologists in the Land of Shinar. For over 150 years after it had been unearthed, it was perceived as a story about how some imaginary gods were born and came to kill each other, in particular, Apsu, the god of fresh water, husband of sea goddess Tiamat, who had transformed into a monster, and the knight who slew her… In this book, we shall prove it a misunderstanding, and that, rather, this epic tale is a highly sophisticated account of how the solar system planets formed, including the Tenth Planet, only recently discovered by mankind. Indeed, contemporary scientific advances validate ancient knowledge, but, on the other hand, it also offers us another way of looking at the history of ancient Near East. It allows us, as we shall demonstrate later, to understand the genetic engineering manipulation used for the Creation of Man, and decipher what the unique Jewish science, Kabbalah, claims to be the hints to hidden knowledge in biblical narratives and throughout the Jewish Classic literature.

—Ben Ami Levavi

CHAPTER 1

IN THE BEGINNING, GOD HATH CREATED

The Kabbalah is in conflict with Jewish Orthodox theology and doctrine, defying the Jewish Orthodox perception of God. According to the kabbalah, the Hebrew Bible is PARDES, literally meaning "garden," but also the Hebrew acronym of *pshat* (literal meaning); *remez* (hint); *drash*, (interpretation); and *sod*, (secret meaning). These are the four possible ways of understanding it: Literal meaning offers hints, which one must examine and interpret, and then secrets are revealed. As our sages stated, he who only studies the literal meaning of the Bible, is better not to study it at all.

The Talmud tells the story of four Jewish scholars who entered the Garden, three of whom were gravely injured: Ben Uzai took a glimpse and died; Ben Zoma took a glimpse and was "injured," that is, lost his mind; Elisha Ben Abuyah, (known by the derogatory term "the other one"), "cut down the trees," that is, absolutely denounced the scripture. Only Rabbi Akiva got in and out of it unscathed. This seems inconceivable: Could one be so seriously injured by words of philosophy, creed, and doctrine, as harsh and uncompromising as they may be? After all, Ben Uzai took a glimpse and died, Ben Zoma went out of his mind, and so forth.

These harsh words are moving and intriguing, and one must find where they originated and why they incurred such grave consequences, to the extent of death and insanity, and find the one or many secrets those three scholars revealed, which had inflicted that unimaginable calamity. So I resolved to go on a quest of examination and interpretation, for hints, in order to reveal the secret. And secrets I did find and revealed… First, I found out that the Hebrew Bible in general and biblical narratives in particular are deeply rooted in the world of Mesopotamian narratives and epic texts of Sumer, or *Shinar*, by its biblical name, depicted on cylinder seals and clay tablets unearthed by archaeologists during the last two centuries and now preserved in museums. To realize fully how all these texts influenced Jewish culture and heritage, we must be acquainted with that era and all its characters that put their stamp on, and left their legacy to the biblical narratives through the numerous scriptures and other epic texts discovered.

One of the greatest epics of the ancient Near East was the Mesopotamian story of creation known as Enuma Elish, a narrative describing, in a most sophisticated manner, the formation of the solar system. Another epic tale is that of Gilgamesh, King of Uruk, or, by its biblical name, *Erech*, and his arduous quest for immortality. In this regard, one must also mention the narrative on the Anunnaki, the equivalent of Nephilim, reported in Chapter 6 of *Genesis* to have landed on Earth about half a million years ago, establishing the first civilizations on our planet. One should also refer to Enki and Ninmah, a text describing the creation of man through genetic engineering manipulation.

The earliest civilization of Mesopotamia, namely the Sumerian, started with the establishment of the First Kingdom of Ur, with Sharu kin. (His names, *sharu* meaning "lord" and *kin* meaning "righteous," are reminiscent of the biblical Malchizedek, "King of Righteousness," in Hebrew.) It was founded on the ruins of an earlier civilization destroyed by the Great Flood. Sumerian epics preceding the Egyptian ones by about 800 years, preserved many cuneiform clay tablets and cylinder seals that tell the story of the earliest era of mankind, and served as the source of inspiration for later Jewish scripture, biblical narratives and Jewish thought. They are so deeply embedded and so strongly hinted in biblical narratives that they can be easily traced to nearly every event narrated in the Pentateuch, the books of the Prophets and even the rest of the Hebrew Bible.

The advancement in technology the last fifty years, particularly the genetic and life science discoveries in general, the discovery of the negative force and the development of electronics, offers mankind a means to grasp the great sophistication and complexity of that epic, which tells, literally, the story of the Creation of the World. It is about the creation of a small world in the great universe, namely the solar system with all its heavenly objects that emerged from Apsu, the all-generating Primordial Sun: all planets near and far, as far as Pluto, including an additional solar system planet, which was definitely the Tenth Planet. The next chapter, "Enuma Elish," includes information on the planet, discovered in 2003 by the Hubble Space Telescope, as well as a photo of a 1987 report on the discovery in *Haaretz* Israeli newspaper and an online report from April 11, 2006 that the Hubble had clearly detected the "tenth planet." That planet, named Nibiru by the Sumerians, is responsible for all known phenomena in the solar system. This Mesopotamian epic also explains several well-known physical phenomena in our solar system. It served to inspire the biblical story of creation written thousands of years later. Definitely, the writers of the Hebrew Bible were well acquainted with the Mesopotamian version, namely the Enuma Elish, from studying the earlier textual documents and cylinder seal images telling the history of the dawn of mankind and civilization on Earth. All these can be easily traced in the biblical narrative, and are an inseparable part of Jewish collective memory since Adam and Eve, through Noah's Flood, Abraham, the Conquest of the Promised Land under Joshua, the establishment of the Kingdom of Israel, and the great wars of the People of Israel with Assyria, Babylonia, Greece and Rome. All these events were affected by the gods, sons of the Nephilim, who had landed on Earth about half a million years ago, coming from a planet recently discovered by mankind, called Nibiru. They had dominated Earth as the Pantheon of twelve self-appointed deities, before leaving Earth about 200 years B.C.E.

The Hebrew Bible starts with the Book of *Genesis*, recounting the creation of heaven and Earth, the solar system with all its planets, the evolution of various animal and vegetable species created by the Word of God; in the Bible's words: and **God saith; God named; God did;** and so on. The name of God recurs 35 times throughout *Genesis* 1 and the beginning of *Genesis* 2, until God "rested from all his work which **God** created and made." Later on, Chapter 2 says, "**Lord God** (Yahweh) made Man."

The difference between **God** and **Lord God**, or Yahweh, is highly significant, just as any other word of the Good Book, as we shall see later on. The biblical creation myth definitely presents two Gods diametrically opposed. The transcendental, invisible, and inconceivable God creates the world, including the solar system, as described in the Story of Creation. He is not the same God who said, "Let us make man in our image, after our likeness," since this God is anthropomorphic, or human-shaped, who can speak and do what he says. He plants a garden east of Eden, placing there the Man he had created. Looking for the source of the biblical writers' knowledge about creation, we must conclude that the biblical creation narrative was inspired by a much earlier Sumerian text, the Enuma Elish creation epic named after its first lines:

Enuma Elish la nabu shamamu

When on high, heaven had not been named,

Shaplitu amatum shuma la zakrat

Down below, firm ground had not been called by name.

This epic, describing the forming of solar system with all its planets, was discovered during the excavation of Nineveh, the seat of Sardanapalus, who reigned from 670 B.C.E. to 620 B.C.E. It was written in cuneiform and translated about a century and a half ago. It is divided into seven tablets, six telling the "narrative" of the creation of our solar system, while the seventh one praises the creator. One cannot help noticing the similarity to the biblical Six Days of Creation, with a seventh day being a day of rest. The tablet Sardanapalus placed at the gate of the library he had named after himself, reads:

The god of scribes endowed me with wisdom and taught me the art of writing; I have learned to read the words of secret, comprehend the hidden engraved on stone, of the days before the Flood."

"[O]n the days before the Flood," over 13,000 years ago, mankind hadn't yet any civilization or culture, and had yet to master the arts of reading and writing. Certainly, at that early age humans could have no notion about the solar system and heavenly bodies, let alone space travels and telecommunication. So, the only explanation for the acquaintance of humans with the planets and zodiacal constellations, which one can read in the so many Sumerian texts, is that it was the legacy of Nephilim who, after the Flood, decided to entrust mankind with controlling its own fate. Thus, they appointed High Priests, serving in temples, to serve as mediators between gods and humans, allowing the gods to reign supreme over humans, as gods should.

"And *God said, Let the waters under the heaven be gathered together unto one place, and let dry land appear*", is a concrete practical command, as opposed to the abstract "**let there be**," such as "***and God said; let there be light***." Here, to follow God's command, water must drain into one place. Since it happened on an Earth that was "without form, and void; and darkness *was* upon the face of the deep" (*Genesis*1:2), one may conclude it was planet Tiamat, "mother of all living things," according to the Sumerian epic, which was originally created as a heavenly body entirely covered by water. Here, the inevitable question is, how could have all the water gathered in one place? What physical phenomenon forced the water to drain, and where did they drain?

The answer to all these questions comes directly from the gods, entities of supreme intelligence, knowledge and wisdom, capable of comprehending cosmic phenomena beyond the understanding of mortals. The legacy they left to mankind contains all the information and knowledge necessary for explaining all the secrets hinted in enigmatic biblical verses. Thus, Enuma Elish, the oldest Creation epic preserved in Sardanapalus' library served, indeed, to inspire the biblical creation narrative, yet it is different from the latter, since in it, the gods did not create, but rather came into being:

*When primordial **Apsu**, their begetter,*
*And **Mummu** and **Tiama**t, she who bore them all*
None of the gods had been brought into being,
And none bore a name, and no destinies determined—
Then it was that the gods were formed in the midst of heaven.
***Lahmu** and **Lahamu** were brought forth, by name they were called.*

Primordial Apsu is the all-generating Sun, out of which all the other heavenly bodies emerged. The word Apsu, reminiscent of "abyss," refers to depth. Here, to the depth of heavens; **Mummu** is Mercury, the planet nearest to the Sun. **Tiamat**, (reminiscent of *Tehomot*, the Hebrew word for "abyss"), is a water-covered planet, mother of all living creatures. The text jumps ahead, presenting Tiamat as planet Earth, as we shall see later on. At that stage, a system of three heavenly bodies was created. "*When…. **no destinies determined***" means that the "destiny," or the position of each heavenly object orbiting around the Sun, had yet to be determined. In other words, that planetary system hadn't settled yet, so the planets were revolving around the Sun in unsteady orbits. *Lahmu and Lahamu*, whose names are similar to *Lohem*, the Hebrew word for "warrior," refer to Mars (god of war), and Venus, who was portrayed as a warrior goddess in Sumer. So now, the solar system had five heavenly bodies. Later on, another five planets appear—making, together with the Sun and the Moon, twelve heavenly bodies.

The Sumerian deities fell under two categories: **Ilu**, "**Gods of Heaven**," the twelve planets of the solar system, as opposed to "**Gods of Heaven and Earth**," the twelve members of the Pantheon. Each of the twelve Gods of Heaven, associated with each of the twelve Gods of Heaven and Earth, members of the Sumerian Pantheon.

This epic offers a most sophisticated description of the forming of the solar system, and accounts for many inexplicable phenomena observed on planet Earth. The epic mentions as many as twelve solar heavenly bodies, namely the Sun, the Moon, then a planet in the making, the nine planets known to us today, and **Nibiru**, an additional planet trapped by the system's gravitation while traveling towards it in the cosmos from the opposite direction. An equivalent of the biblical **draining of water** is described in Tablet IV, titled the **Celestial Battle**: planet Nibiru, by its Sumerian name, (the later Assyro-Babylonian god Bel-Marduk, or the Jewish Yahweh/Lord), collided with Tiamat, halving her. The half of her that suffered the impact was scattered all around, turning into the asteroid belt, or firmament. The other half was pushed towards the current position of the Moon. The latter was caught by Tiamat's gravity, and became its satellite. In the biblical narrative, God made "…**the lesser light to rule the night**" (*Genesis* 1:16). The water, which had covered Tiamat in the beginning of Creation, was drained into the space created in the surviving half, thus forming the oceans. At its other end, land appeared and continents were formed, thus turning the surviving half of Tiamat into planet Earth.

Here is a translation of the Celestial Battle scene in Tablet IV:

Then Tiamat and Marduk joined issue, wisest of gods.
They strove in single combat, locked in battle.
The lord spread out his net to enfold her,
The Evil Wind, which followed behind, he let loose in her face.

The lord trod on the legs of Tiamat,
With his unsparing mace he crushed her skull.

When the arteries of her blood he had severed,
The North Wind bore it to places undisclosed.

"**Her blood**" born to places undisclosed refers to the comets, the pieces of Tiamat's former satellites scattered at all directions, which return to their original location irregularly. Unlike them, the scattered parts of Tiamat are the asteroids, which keep revolving at Tiamat's previous location, between Mars and Jupiter. Other phenomenon explained by the Celestial Battle are the reverse direction of the Earth's rotation, since it is the only solar system planet revolving clockwise; the inclination of Earth axis, due to that collision; and finally, the migration of sources of life from Nibiru to Earth, as a direct consequence of the collision.

> The following table lists the solar system's heavenly bodies as referred to in Enuma Elish: the first column on the right lists the Sumerian names of twelve Gods of Heaven, or solar system's heavenly bodies; the column next to it, the names of the corresponding twelve members of Sumerian Pantheon; next to it, the name of the corresponding planet. The last on that list is Bel/Marduk/Lord, the chief deity of the Babylonians; the same chief deity of *Ashur* ("seer," in Assyrian), by the Assyrians. Their planet was Nibiru, the tenth planet. Next to them are the current names of the planets.

	God of Heaven	God of Heaven and Earth	Planet
1	Apsu	Utu/Shammash	Sol/Helios/Sun
2	Mummu	Ishkur/Hadad	Mercury
3	Tiamat	Enlil	Terra/Earth/Gaia
4	Lahmu	Nabu	Mars
5	Lahamu	Ishtar	Venus
6	Anshar	Ninurta	Saturn
7	Kishar	Nergal	Jupiter
8	Anu	Anu/An	Uranus
9	Nudimmud	Enki/ Ea	Neptune
10	Kingu	Nanar/Sin	Moon/Luna
11	Gaga	Tamuz	Pluto
12	Nibiru	Bel/Marduk/Lord Yahweh	Marduk

Table 1

To conclude, this chapter is about the One and Only God, Creator of Heaven and Earth, and about another two kinds of deities: **Gods of Heaven**, which are all the heavenly bodies of the solar system, and **Gods of Heaven and Earth**, members of the Sumerian Pantheon, each of whom is associated with one of the Gods of Heaven.

Being acquainted with the names of various Gods of Heaven and Earth, that is, the twelve members of Sumerian Pantheon, as well as the twelve Gods of Heaven, or the solar system's bodies, we can better interpret the Creation Epic of Enuma Elish, discussed in the next chapter.

CHAPTER 2

ENUMA ELISH | EPIC OF CREATION

The epic Enuma Elish, was named after its initial Akkadian words were written in cuneiform on clay tablets, discovered by archaeologists in Mesopotamia, Iraq and Iran.

For over a century and a half since then, numerous tablets, pictures, illustrations and cylinder stamps have been discovered and deciphered, shedding new light on these unearthed messages. Most of the findings were from the great libraries of Nineveh and Nippur, each of which contained over twenty-five thousand tablets. Texts found in other Sumerian and Akkadian site ruins, too, have been deciphered and translated. All these discoveries shed new light on many ancient pieces of knowledge dealing with the natural sciences, particularly genetics, electronics, and space, which mankind only managed to understand at the second half of the 20th century.

The events recorded by ancient historical texts were initially related as oral traditions through the ages, when writing was only mastered by the privileged few. No doubt, over time these stories were blended with fantasies and distortions that make no sense, at face value, without an unshakable religious conviction. Since these texts, written in cuneiform on clay tablets, are the oldest versions recorded and preserved, they can serve as a reliable source of information for further study on both the scriptures and the earliest history of planet Earth and mankind.

A Hebrew rendition of Enuma Elish from the Greek by Shaul Tchernichovsky was published as early as 1937. The same poet also masterfully translated classical epic Egyptian, Greek, and Roman works, plus other literature, into Hebrew holding a proud place in the Hebrew poetry pantheon. Yet even he admitted in his notes to his translation that he had failed to comprehend the meaning of certain names and expressions, which seem clearer now. The next chapter includes the full text of the epic, with explanations based on the most recent archaeological discoveries.

Astronomers, physicists, and other scientists engaged in space studies have been arguing for a while that our solar system has a tenth planet, in addition to the nine already known, namely Mercury, the closest to the Sun, and Venus, are the inner planets; i.e., between the Sun and the Earth. Next to them are Earth and Mars, making four planets together; next are Jupiter and Saturn, the two largest of all, making the fifth and sixth planets from the Sun, (the volume of Saturn is 800 times that of Earth, and Jupiter, 1300 times Earth); Uranus and Neptune make the seventh and eighth planets, with Pluto being the ninth.

But what about the tenth planet?

Mankind only learned about the farthest planets fairly recently; Uranus was discovered as late as 1781, Neptune, in 1846, and the existence of Pluto was deducted from calculations in 1930. The solar system as we know it today, is shown in Illustration 1, in which the distance between the Sun and planets is presented approximately.

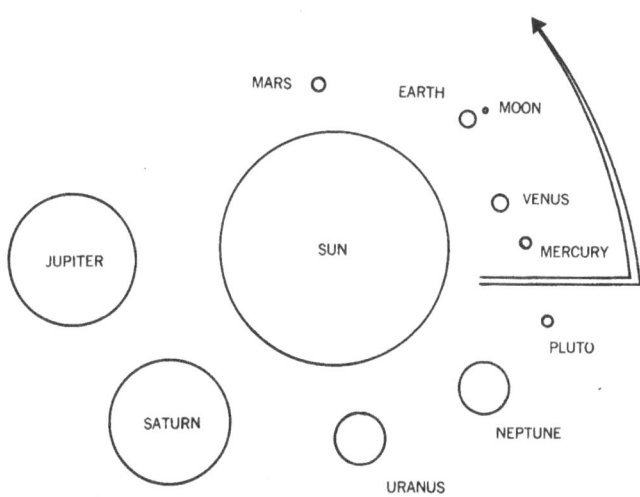

Illustration 1: The solar system according to Enuma Elish, yet with ten bodies.

The illustration above shows there is a great distance between Mars and Jupiter, where the asteroid belt is situated. The arrow shows the revolution direction around the Sun. The Moon is shown near Earth. According to scientists, when the events took place, the Moon was a planet in the making, and therefore was considered a significant heavenly object and played an important part in the Mesopotamian creation story. The inevitable conclusion is that there must be another planet responsible, or which had previously caused the presence of asteroid belt there. Indeed, the discovery of a tenth planet was reported online in 2006:

[Tuesday, April 11, 2006] For the first time, NASA's Hubble Space Telescope has seen distinctly the "tenth planet," currently nicknamed "Xena," and has found that it is only slightly larger than Pluto.

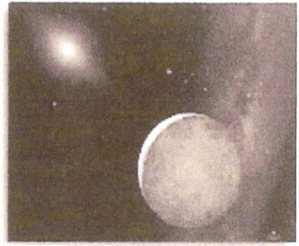

Picture A

That ancient planet, discovered by the Hubble Space Telescope, was named "Xena." It is a very old planet, the discovery of which asserts the existence of other planets of other solar systems. Another increasingly prevailing scientific theory is that planets with a solar system had been blown apart, projecting one planet to travel in space. Scientists concluded that the forming of planets was a much more expansive and earlier process than once assumed. Moreover, in the words of a US team of researchers, "the existence of ancient planets means that life started between five and six billion years earlier than first estimated by astronomers and other scientists." One may say life started in space long before it emerged on Earth. Most interestingly, all these supposedly recent discoveries had already been known to our ancestors, millennia ago, and are shown in artifacts such as texts, cylinder seals and stone inscriptions discovered by archaeologists throughout the Ancient World and only deciphered and translated recently. The Seed of Life, known as DNA, was brought to our solar system by the invading planet **Nibiru**, by the Sumerians and **Marduk** by the Babylonians, and transferred to Earth because of a collision with a planet called **Tiamat**, part of which became planet Earth. As Zecharia Sitchin, author of *The Twelfth Planet*, argues the Sumerian cosmogony claimed our solar system to have originated from an errant planet close to the Sun, namely **Mercury**, and another, larger planet, called **Tiamat**, a water-covered planet, orbiting where the asteroid belt is currently situated. Next, the two planets, **Mars** and **Venus**, situated around the Sun, were created, and later on, the pairs of planets **Jupiter** and **Saturn**, **Uranus** and **Neptune**. They were joined by another planet, projected into space and attracted by the solar system's gravitational pull, and has been revolving around it in a distant elliptical orbit.

Garden of Secrets 11

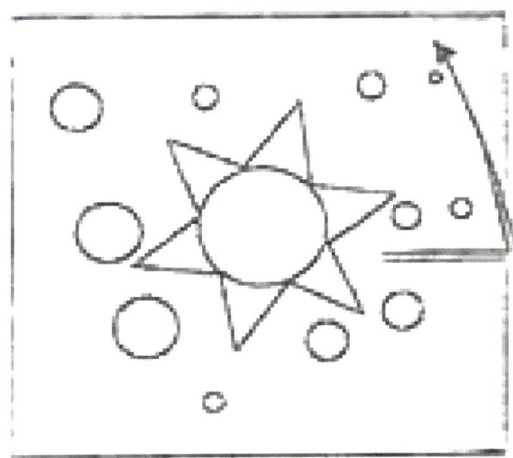

Illustration 2: A 4000 years cylinder seal (Berlin artifact no. VA/243) showing a god seated and two goddesses standing; between the goddesses, there is a large circle with smaller circles around it, representing the solar system planets. One can notice another planet between Mars and Jupiter, where Tiamat was situated before the collision.

The invading planet **Nibiru/Marduk**, attracted to the center of the solar system by gravity, moved in a direction making it collide with Tiamat, which, at that time, was a totally water-covered planet. As a result of that collision, half of Tiamat was scattered into space, and started orbiting around the Sun as an asteroid belt. Its other half, as the biblical creation story reads, "***And God said, Let the waters under the heaven be gathered together unto one place, and let the dry land appear***" (*Genesis*1:9). The water covering Tiamat was gathered into the void, that other half which had survived the collision, and dry land appeared. Thus, Tiamat came to be planet Earth, driven by the collision into another orbit, closer to the Moon, which, caught by Earth's gravitational pull, became its satellite. This cosmological event offers a reasonable explanation for the oceans being situated on one side of the globe, while the continents are on the other side. Indeed, the **Enuma Elish** is no myth, as scholars have assumed since its discovery. Rather, this epic is a most allegorical description of the formation of the solar system. This event, referred to in the Sumerian culture as the **Celestial Battle**, was fought by all the Gods of Heaven (as heavenly bodies were referred to by the ancient people. This was to distinguish them from the twelve Gods of Heaven and Earth - the members of the Pantheon, discussed later in Chapter 4). The invading planet was **Nibiru**, God of Heaven by its Sumerian version of the epic, or **Marduk**, in the Babylonian version. According to the texts, this planet was made in the deep heavens, in the "*Assembly of Destinies*," and then projected into space, and, attracted by the solar system's gravitational pull, joined it in a distant elliptical orbit.

This cosmic cataclysm took place in an early age, while the combustion of the newborn Sun generated explosions and projected great mass into space. Large masses attracted the smaller ones that gradually formed the planets orbiting around the Sun. Yet their orbits were still unstable, with the heavenly bodies moving too close to each other, risking collision. "***Their waters joining, becoming one***." Then, "***the gods joined in alliance***," deciding to fight Tiamat, asking Nibiru/Marduk to undertake this task. Once the gods accept his demands, planet Marduk approached Tiamat, hitting and halving her, thus stabilizing the solar system, starting all the known peculiar behaviors of planet Earth: the inclination of its axis, accounting for the change of seasons; the reversed direction of rotation, clockwise, as opposed to all other planets; the dispersion of the damaged half of Tiamat formed the asteroid belt between Mars and Jupiter; the projection of Tiamat towards the Moon and imprisoned it as a satellite; and the moving of elements of life from the impacting Nibiru to the impacted Tiamat, which came to be planet Earth, "***who bore them all***," in the epic's words.

Until recently, the Bible was the only source of information on early human history. In the early twentieth century, archaeology was still in its infancy, the scholars specializing in these disciplines were few, and many discovered texts had still to be deciphered. The is recent comprehension and publication of cuneiform tablets found in Shinar with especially abundant material dating from late Ur dynasties' period 5th to late 2nd millennia B.C.E. Alongside recent technologies, namely electronic telescopes and microscopes, allow us nowadays to see the ancient Near Eastern history more clearly, and to better understand the means and powers used by the ancients. So, one may assume it was the cuneiform clay tablets preserved in the great libraries of ancient rulers that were the source of biblical narratives, which were transmitted orally through the ages when writing was an uncommon act, before they were collected at later periods.

In the early 19th century, archaeologist Henry Austen Layard excavated the ruins of Nineveh, one of the seven earliest cities established on the banks of the Tigris, the same Nineveh referred to in *Jonah* 1:2: "**Arise, go to Nineveh, that great city, and cry against it.**" From 670 B.C.E. to 620 B.C.E., ruled by Sardanapalus, a man of letters. In a tablet found in the city, he states he had studied and even cared to preserve records "on the days before the Flood." The library unearthed in his palace basement contained over twenty-five thousand clay tablets, arranged by subject, encompassing any subject on which a person might think. In the city of Nippur, by the Persian Gulf, another of those seven early cities, a library of similar capacity was discovered. Western museum archaeologists retrieved the contents of such libraries. They demonstrate that the art of writing was mastered in Sumerian and Elamite kingdoms in very early periods, which made these countries the centers of culture, knowledge, technology and civilization of ancient Near East.

Clay tablets, well preserved in the libraries of Nineveh, Nippur, Mari and other cities, before being unearthed by archaeologists, left mankind an abundance of literary works such as epics, as well as documents and texts dealing with all aspects of human life. These texts reveal an advanced knowledge in the fields of astronomy and other space sciences, electronics, and genetics, to the amazement and puzzlement of modern society. As said, the ancients regarded all solar system heavenly bodies as gods, Gods of Heaven, especially due to their effect, for better or for worse, on a person's future. The Akkadians believed the changes of planets mass and the duration of their revolution around the Sun significantly affected the fates of human communities, and that acquaintance with these past changes allows one to foretell what time has in store. After all, natural cataclysms such as floods, or extinctions of animal species, were brought about by such changes. Zecharia Sitchin, who analyzed Mesopotamian cuneiform texts, argues in his book *The Twelfth Planet* that the Flood, which took place about 13000 years ago, started because planet Nibiru came too close to Earth while orbiting the Sun. It took place late in the Ice Age, when the pressure of the glaciers on the ground created a slippery surface. The proximity of Nibiru, with its strong gravity, accelerated the process, making the glaciers slide suddenly into the ocean, thus raising the level of water that, in turn, covered the land.

Not incidentally did the astronomers name the recently discovered planet on the edge of the solar system after **Methuselah**, father of Lamech and grandfather of Noah, man of the Flood. According to *Genesis* 6:22, he was one of the ten ancestors of mankind. There are many texts from Sumer, biblical Shinar, referring to Nibiru, the planet with an elliptical orbit, one end of which is far in deep space, while another end is near the Sun. In the beautiful words of *Psalms*: "**Which is *as a bridegroom coming out of his canopy,* and *rejoiceth as a hero to run a race; His going forth* is *from the edge of the heaven, and his circuit unto the ends of it: and there is nothing hidden from his rage*"** (*Psalms* 19:5-6). A recently discovered fragment of the **Enuma Elish** creation story presents it as a planet formed in deep space, in the "Assembly of Destinies," caught by solar system gravity, thus becoming a solar system body periodically revolving around the Sun.

Moon, or **Kingu**, was also considered a god of heaven, and is listed as a "full member" of the twelve planets group. Scientists, who argue that initially the Moon was a planet in the making, share this concept. Being the largest of the numerous satellites of the solar system, it had its own gravity, which, though rather weak, was strong enough to attract space particles. Thus the Moon grew larger, and was about to start its own orbit around the Sun, "tablet of destinies" in the words of the ancients. Many pictures, taken by NASA's Apollo space mission, showed vast craters on the Moon created by impacts with bodies of various sizes. The examination of lunar soil samples, too, reveals that in ancient times, the Moon had undergone melting and inner movement processes, as other planets had.

The ancients were well acquainted with the solar system, with the size and position of every orbiting planet, and knew about Jupiter and Saturn, the two largest planets. Yet the main discovery by the Enuma Elish was the existence of another solar system planet, reported in ancient texts, pictures, cylinder stamps and inscribed stones. The ancients reported two major facts on this planet: it was habitable, and space-traveling creatures settled there ages ago, traveling with it through the solar system, approaching Earth and exploring its living conditions.

Landing on Earth, they established the very first civilization, the history of which this book tells through texts and pictures written on cylinder seals and clay tablets discovered and deciphered during the last one hundred and fifty years.

The process of creation presented as the Celestial Battle, fought between the Gods of Heaven, or the twelve major heavenly bodies of the early solar system. At that stage, it was still unstable, with the planets being formed from matter projected into space by explosions on the Sun, moving too close to one another, risking a collision. The epic reports these events through personification, turning the actors into Gods of Heaven who, plotting, thinking, and consulting, make fatal decisions.

The epic was discovered by archaeologists in Mesopotamia, the biblical Shinar, the land between the Tigris and Euphrates, written in cuneiform on clay tablets. It is divided into six tablets, or chapters, describing six days of creation, and another tablet of praise. This is similar to the biblical creation narrative, with six days of creation and a seventh day of rest. Just as in **Enuma Elish**, the biblical creation story deals with heavenly bodies, namely the Sun, Moon and stars, and the waters above, and the waters under the heaven. On a closer look, one can see the biblical story as allusive and allegorical, avoiding explanations of what was going on, since its ultimate purpose is the exaltation of the acts of God. He is the only one who **creates** with his words: "***And God said, Let there be a firmament in the midst of the waters,- and let it differ water of above from water below***"; (*Genesis* 1:6); the one who **makes**: "***And God made two great lights***" (*Genesis* 1:16); the one who **sets:** "***And God set them in the firmament of the heaven to give light upon the Earth***," (*Genesis*1:17) and **so on…** By comparison, Enuma Elish is not about praising a god. Though it deals with deities, namely Gods of Heaven, who are, as we said, all heavenly bodies of the solar system, they act by being creatures of the Sun, "***primordial Apsu, their begetter***" (Apsu, reminiscent of "abyss," means here "the depth of heaven"). The only explanation for their being and their arrangement in the solar system is cosmic events: First, they were formed as a result of solar eruptions on primordial Apsu, "their begetter;" second, an intrusion of a large planet from space; third, its collision with Tiamat, one of the earliest planets to have been formed out of the matter projected from the Sun.

There are two versions of the epic: an earlier one, in Sumerian, and later, in Akkadian. The Sumerian versions had many fissures and gaps, but it was possible to fully reconstruct with segments of its later version. The Babylonian version parallels the Celestial Battle to the hard struggle between Marduk, the Babylonian chief deity, and other deities, over whom he triumphed. Eventually, he had been made the dominant deity at the end of second millennium or early first millennium B.C.E., when planet Nibiru was renamed Marduk, after the king of the twelve members of Sumerian, Akkadian and Babylonian Pantheon.

Until nearly seventy years ago, when many Mesopotamian texts had yet to be deciphered and translated, the Enuma Elish Creation Epic, as many other myths of antiquity, has been puzzling students of ancient Near Eastern civilizations. Today, due to the deciphering and translation of many discovered texts and other documents, and, mostly, due to the technological progress of the last five decades, humanity has the means to better understand the practical meaning, amazing amount of knowledge, and the significant message the ancients had left us. Only today can we understand the distinction in the epic of the Gods of Heaven, which are all major solar system elements, and the Gods of Heaven and Earth, who are the twelve members of the Sumerian Pantheon, each of the latter gods was allotted one of the twelve planets.

ENUMA ELISH LA NABU

SHMMAMU

**When on heights Heaven had
not been named**

SHAPLITU AMMATUM

SHUMMA LA ZAKRAT

**Below, firm ground had
not been called by name**

The Akkadian Epic, Enuma Elish, named after its initial words, was written in cuneiform on clay tablets discovered by archaeologists in Mesopotamia, contemporary Iraq and Iran.

Tablet I
The creation of the world;

Gods are formed, and decide to make war on Tiamat:

When in heights, heaven had not been named,
below, Earth had not been called by name;
When primordial Apsu, their begetter,
And Mummu and Tiamat, she who bore them all,
Their waters were mingled together.

No reed hut had sprung forth, no marshland had appeared,
None of the gods had been brought into being,
And none bore a name, and no destinies determined
Then it was that the gods were formed in the midst.
Lahmu and Lahamu were brought forth,

Before they had grown in age and stature,
Anshar and Kishar were formed, surpassing the others.
Long were the days, multiplied the years,
Anu was born, their heir, of his fathers the rival;
Yes, Anshar's first-born, Anu, was his equal.
Anu begot Nudimmud in his image.
This Nudimmud was of his fathers the master;
Of broad wisdom, understanding, mighty in strength,
Mightier by far than his grandfather, Anshar.
He had no rival among the gods, his brothers.

Thus were the great gods joined in alliance,
Disturbing Tiamat, Derided her guardians;…

"*[P]rimordial Apsu, their begetter*" refers to the then Sun, the beginning of everything, out of which all other heavenly bodies emerged. *Apsu* or *Absu*, reminiscent of "abyss," means "depth," either deep water or deep space. Here, is refers to the Sun in the depths of heaven. At this stage, one can imagine the Sun as just created, undergoing a series of eruptions, projecting matter into space, a matter forming, associating particles and turning into planets.

"*Mummu*" is Mercury, the planet closest to the Sun. **Tiamat**: The Mother of All Living, the text runs ahead of events. At this stage, Tiamat, reminiscent of "*tehomot*," the Hebrew word for "deep," is a water-covered planet, which eventually becomes life-bearing planet Earth, mother of all living.

"*Their waters mingled together*," means that due to excessive proximity between heavenly bodies in the early stages of creation, waters from different heavenly bodies "mingled" together, by gravitational forces.

"*None of the gods…and no destinies determined*" As we said, the ancients considered all heavenly bodies to be Gods of Heaven. "Destinies" refers to the specific orbit of each planet, which is its "Fate and Destiny."

"*Lahmu and Lahamu were brought forth*": Lahmu and Lahamu, whose names are similar to Lohem, Hebrew word for "warrior," are Mars (god of war), and Venus, a Sumerian warrior goddess revered for terrorizing all her rivals.

"*Anshar and Kishar were formed, surpassing the others!*": Anshar and Kishar are Saturn and Jupiter. The ancients were so well acquainted with the solar system, that they mention these are the two largest of its planets: the volume of Saturn is nearly 800 times that of Planet Earth; that of Jupiter is 1300 times that of planet Earth.

"*Anu begot Nudimmud in his image*": This refers to Uranus and Neptune. Nudimmud is the pet name of Enki/Ea, and the name of one of the Gods of Heaven and Earth, as we shall see later.

"*Thus were….joined in alliance*": Banded against the watchers, sons of gods – the eleven satellites circled Tiamat in the beginning, endangering all around.

And Tiamat was speechless at their ways.
Their doings were loathsome unto....
Their way was evil; they were overbearing.
Then Apsu, the begetter of the great gods,
Cried out, addressing Mummu, his minister:

"O Mummu, my vizier, who rejoices my spirit,
Come here and let us go to Tiamat!"
They went and sat down before Tiamat,
conspiring against the gods, their first-born.
Apsu, opening his mouth,
Said to resplendent Tiamat:
"Their ways are truly loathsome to me.
By day I find no relief, nor repose by night.
I will destroy, I will wreck their ways,
That quiet may be restored. Let us have rest!"

As soon as Tiamat heard this,
She was furious and called out aloud.
She cried out aggrieved, as she raged all alone,
She uttered a curse, and unto Apsu she spoke:

"What? Should we destroy that which we have built?"

Then Mummu answered, giving counsel to Apsu;
Ill-wishing and ungracious was Mummu's advice...

"*Thus were the great gods joined in an alliance, They disturbed Tiamat as they surged back and forth.*" The eleven satellites Tiamat had in the early stages of creation used to revolve in a disordered way, threatening a general collision. At this stage, an early unstable solar system came into being, with nine heavenly bodies, with the Sun in its center and eight planets, formed in pairs, which were revolving around the Sun at dangerously close orbits.

"*Yes, **they troubled the bosom of Tiamat***": The planets came so close to Tiamat, that their gravities started streaming in the water of Tiamat, unsettling orbits of the planets around the Sun. Therefore, Absu and Mummu undertook to address Tiamat with their plan of restoring peace. "**Counseling against the gods, *their first-born***": they assembled to annihilate the sons of gods, That is, the eleven satellites Tiamat had in the early stages of Creation. As usual in case of declaration of war, the threatened party did not concede easily: as a result of the words which Apsu communicated to Tiamat, "**She was furious and called out…**", scheming to fight back and subdue her eight opponents, who had conspired against her, in order to reign supreme over them, thus foiling their schemes of destroying the sons of gods, her guardians.

Now, one can clearly understand what that epic, which is a dramatic report on the formation of the solar system, following their attributes: "**Primordial Apsu, the begetter of them all**"; Tiamat, "***who bore them all***"; the two greatest planets of the system, Anshar and Kishar; the order in which the planets emerged and the positions of their orbits around the Sun. In the process of the emergence of the three missing heavenly bodies, we can see, with increasing clarity, the entire solar system as we know it. Many of the solar system's heavenly body's names are hinted at in the numerous texts dealing with this subject, including Uranus, referred to as "Anu," and Neptune, referred to as "Nudimmud." Once again, one is amazed by the extent of ancient knowledge, knowing that Uranus was discovered as late as 1781, and Neptune, in 1846. Therefore, the inevitable question is: how could the ancients, living thousands of years ago, have such detailed information? Who might have taught early mankind such complex and unfathomable knowledge that we have only recently acquired? Let us bear in mind that Copernicus published his heliocentric theory, disproving the church's claim that the Earth is the center of the universe, as late as 1453 B.C.E.

"*Then **Mummu answered, giving counsel to Apsu***": Mummu, that is, Mercury, the closest planet to the Sun, is not impressed by Tiamat's cry. Being belligerent, he gives Apsu his ill-wishing advice. Mercury, presented here as the errant planet of the Sun, offers to destroy the sons of the gods:

"Do destroy, my father, the mutinous ways.
Then you will have relief by day and rest by night!"

When Apsu heard this, his face grew radiant
Because of the evil he planned against the gods, his sons.
As for Mummu, he embraced him by the neck
As that one sat down on his knees to kiss him.

They banded themselves and marched at the side of Tiamat.
Enraged, they plot without cease night and day,
They are set for combat, growling, raging
They form a council to prepare for the fight.

Mother of chaos, she who fashions all things,
Added matchless weapons, bore monster-serpents,
Sharp of tooth, unsparing of fang.
With venom for blood she has filled their bodies.
Roaring dragons she has clothed with terror,
Has crowned them with haloes, making them like gods,
Whoever beheld them, terror overcame him,
And that, with their bodies reared up none might turn them back.

She set up a Viper, a Dragon, a monster,
A Great-Lion, a Mad-Dog, and a Scorpion-Man,
Mighty lion-demons, a Dragon-Fly, a Centaur—
Bearing weapons that do not spare, fearless in battle.

"*Do destroy, my father, the mutinous ways*";

These words of Mummu addressed to Apsu, and Apsu's approval, actually tipped the scale in favor of war, thus dooming "the sons of gods," Tiamat's protectors.

The author of this drama portrays the two hosts about to engage in battle: one host is Apsu, who initiated the war, and Mummu, who encourages him and six of the planets; opposing them is Tiamat with her eleven protectors, sons of gods. In other words, on one side were eight of the heavenly bodies making the early, unstable solar system, while opposite it, were Tiamat and the eleven satellites orbiting it most chaotically, threatening to destroy the entire solar system. Tiamat's response could have surprised even the greatest skeptics: though she might have cried and had her schemes, yet once realizing that Apsu had doomed the sons of gods, her protectors, they band and march together, "**Enraged, they plot, set for combat, growling, raging.**"

She is called "mother of chaos" because, later on, Ea tells Anshar the plots of Tiamat, accusing her of preparing a war which would end up in a chaos and universal disorder.

"**[S]*he who fashions all things*": Tiamat is the only body of the solar system where animals and plants were created. It is here, on Earth, that life emerged, where the entire universe is. Therefore, all the events of this creation epic are associated with the actions of Tiamat. Her very name, *Ti*, meaning "life," and *Amat*, meaning "Earth," means she is "Land of the Livings."

All further reports on Tiamat's deeds perfectly account for the consequences of heavenly bodies orbiting too dangerously close to one another, intersecting courses and hitting one another. The powerful gravitational pull of Tiamat generated electrical emanations, manifested as lightning and thunderstorms, whirling winds and total turbulence: she "**Added matchless weapons, bore monster-serpents,... Roaring dragons she has clothed with terror, Has crowned them with haloes,**[...]"

And now we are in for the big surprise when Tiamat takes the most reckless action. Preparing her eleven satellites for battle, and interfering with creation, an action which no god of heaven could have accepted:

Bearing weapons that do not spare, fearless in battle.
Her decrees were firm, they were beyond resisting.

All together eleven of this kind she brought forth.

From among the gods, her first-born, who formed her Assembly,
She elevated Kingu, made him chief among them.

The leading of the ranks, command of the Assembly,
The raising of weapons for the encounter, advancing to combat,
To direct the battle, to control the fight,
These she entrusted to his hand as she seated him in the Council:
"I have cast for you the spell, exalting you in the Assembly of the gods.
To counsel all the gods I have given you full power.

Truly, you are supreme, you are my only consort!
Your utterance shall prevail over all the Anunnaki!"
She gave him the Tablet of Destinies, fastened on his breast:
"As for you, your command shall be unchangeable your word shall endure!"
As soon as Kingu was elevated, possessed of the rank of Anu,
They decreed the fate for the gods, his sons:

"Your word shall make the fire subside,
Shall humble the 'Power-Weapon,' so potent in its sweep!"

[Tablet II]

When Tiamat had thus lent import to her handiwork,
She prepared for battle against the gods, her offspring.

To avenge Apsu, Tiamat planned evil.

That she was girding for battle was divulged to Ea.

As soon as Ea heard of this matter,

He lapsed into dark silence and sat still.

The days went by, and his anger subsided.

"*She elevated Kingu,*" refers to the Moon. As mentioned above, scientists consider the Moon at stage to have been a planet in the making, gaining weight from matter accumulated from outer space, and drifting away from Earth into an orbit of its own around the Sun; in the words of the ancients, "tablet of destinies."

"*She made him chief among them.*

The leading of the ranks, command of the Assembly."

This was Tiamat's original scheme, to reign supreme. It was to this purpose that she made him "counsel to the gods," and gave him full power. So, Kingu assumes his position, he starts commanding the gods, giving them their "fates," that batter assignments.

Kingu, or Sin, by his Akkadian name, made the tenth solar system body; his ascent to the supreme switches the plot diametrically. Realizing that war is imminent, the gods attempt to make a different move.

The author endows the solar system bodies with the human capabilities of thinking, planning, consulting, as well as with human motivations. Analyzing the state of things at this stage, one may conclude:

a. Mummu, the groveling errant of Apsu, the Sun, was excited by the atmosphere, offering Apsu to threaten Tiamat: Apsu fell for his advice, thus dooming the sons of gods.

b. Tiamat assesses her opponents, the warlike Lahmu and Lahamu; the pair Anshar and Kishar, "surpassing the others"; and another pair, Anu and Nudimmud, no poor shots either, are two planets far larger than Tiamat. Yet she is resolved to make challenging moves, surprising the alliance of gods.

c. As we shall see later on, Ea/Enki, Nudimmud takes his own initiative.

Tablet II

"Ea" means "water dweller"; Enki means "lord of the Earth" while Nudimmud is his pet name.

He went to Anshar, his fore father.
When he came before his grandfather, Anshar,
He repeated all that Tiamat had plotted to him

"Our mother Tiamat, she who bore us, detests us.
She has set up the Assembly and is furious with rage.
All the gods have rallied to her;
Even those whom you brought forth march at her side.
They throng and march at the side of Tiamat,
Enraged, they plot without cease night and day.
They are set for combat, growling, raging,
They have formed a council to prepare for the fight.
Mother Hubur, she who fashions all things,
Has added matchless weapons, has born monster-serpents,

Sharp of tooth, unsparing of fang.
With venom for blood she has filled their bodies.
Roaring dragons she has clothed with terror,
Has crowned them with haloes, making them like gods,
So that he who beholds them is overcome by terror,
Their bodies rear up and none can withstand their attack.
She has set up a Vipers Dragon, and a Sphinx,
A Great-Lion, a Mad-Dog, and a Scorpion-Man,
Mighty lion-demons, a Dragon-Fly, a Centaur—
Bearing weapons that spare not, fearless in battle.

Her decrees are firm, they are beyond resisting.
All together eleven of this kind she has brought forth.
From among the gods, her first-born who formed her Assembly,
She has elevated Kingu, has made him chief among them.

When Ea *"went to Anshar, his fore father,"* telling him what Tiamat had plotted, and that *"**All the gods have rallied to her; Even those whom you brought forth march at her side**,"* he refers to the sons of gods, the satellites. This indicates that some gods supported Tiamat. Indeed, later we read that Ea out-debated Mummu and Apsu, which indicates disputes within that alliance about the proper way to act, Ea differing with Mummu and Apsu. As it seems, Ea's suggestion was accepted eventually. Here, he repeats the same words that concluded Tablet I: *"**They throng and march at the side of Tiamat**."* This was a Sumerian, and, later, an Akkadian and Babylonian literary tradition. The repetition of words, and even long segments, was to inspire the reader with the feeling of events. Moreover, the narrator always concludes with some of his own phrases, thus expanding the plot and driving it into the reader's mind. The words of Ea are concluded with the words of Kingu in the next page:

"Your word shall make the fire subside,
Shall humble the 'Power-Weapon,' so potent in its sweep!"

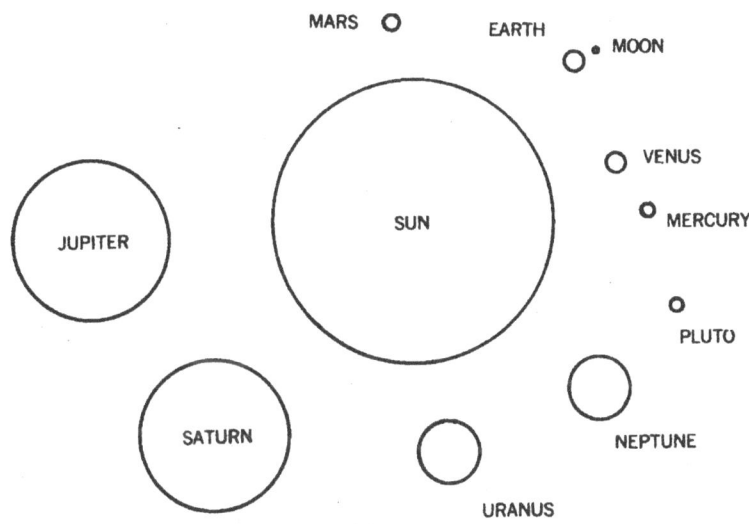

Illustration 3: The solar system according to Enuma Elish, yet with 10 bodies.

To direct the battle, to control the fight,
She entrusted these to his hands as she seated him in the Council:
I have cast the spell for you, exalting you in the Assembly of the gods.
To counsel all the gods I have given you full power.

Truly, you are supreme, you are my only consort!
Your utterance shall prevail over all the Anunnaki!'
She has given him the Tablet of Destinies, fastened on his breast:
'As for you, your command shall be unchangeable, your word shall endure!'
As soon as Kingu was elevated, possessed of the rank of Anu,
They decreed the fate for the gods, her sons:
'Your word shall make the fire subside,
Shall humble the "Power-Weapon," so potent in its sweep!'
When Anshar heard that Tiamat was sorely troubled,
He struck his loins and bit his lips.

His heart was gloomy, his mood restless.
He covered his mouth to stifle his outcry:

"Ea, my son, wage war! Take up arms, mighty one!

Lo, you came over Mummu and Apsu.
Now, submis Kingu, who marches before her.

He addressed a word to Anu, his son:
"Anu my son,... mighty hero,...
Whose strength is outstanding, his onslaught cannot be withstood.
Go and stand before Tiamat,
That her mood be calmed, that her heart may be merciful.

Tiamat's vigorous actions had an unexpected effect. Reading the words Ea repeated to Anshar, it feels as if war is imminent, especially after she had "*elevated Kingu.....To direct the battle, to control the fight*," and, in the epic's words, "*given him the Tablet of Destinies, fastened on his breast.*" (That is to say, gave him his own orbit in the system). Once appointed a supreme commander, Kingu loses no time, setting for the gods their assignments.

Hearing the detailed report about Tiamat's action, which definitely made a great tumult, Anshar was "sorely troubled," but giving it another thought, he calmed down, "*He covered his mouth to stifle his outcry*," addressing Ea: "*Lo, you submised Mummu and Apsu. Now, go submis Kingu, who marches before her.*"

Later on, the tablet is altered and there is a discontinuity between this stanza and the next one. According to Tchernichovsky's note, it probably describes the horror that befell Ea. However, Anshar bids Anu: "*Go and stand before Tiamat*," in an attempt to soothe her.

The next page is altered too, but later on, another heavenly body is mentioned, a planet called "Marduk," formed in deep space, which plays a highly significant role in the later plot.

Usually, planets were depicted in cylinder stamps and clay tablets as symbols, allowing recognized by their physical features. Illustration 4 shows on the left the crescent, the shape of the rising Moon in the beginning of the month; it symbolizes Kingu/Sin, or the Moon, then a planet in the making. In the middle, there is the symbol of Nibiru/Marduk, a cross inside a circle, which stands for the Planet of Crossing, since its orbit around the Sun crosses the solar system. (This is reminiscent of the Star of Bethlehem and the Cross, which came to symbolize Christianity.) The heat lines emerging between the beams of the cross indicate that Nibiru is a large planet, emitting heat from its center. On the right, there is planet Lahamu, or Venus, the 8th planet from the outside of the solar system, symbolized by an eight-beamed star.

 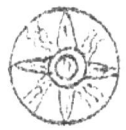 

Illustration 4

If she will not listen to your word,
Then tell her our word, that she might be calmed."

When he heard the command of his father, Anshar,
He made straight for her way, following the road to her.

But when Anu was near enough to see the plan of Tiamat,
He was not able to face her and he turned back.

"Marduk, my son, heed to thy father's word!
For you are my son who comforts his heart.
When facing Anshar, approach as though in combat;
Stand up as you speak; seeing you, he will grow restful."
The lord rejoiced at the word of his father;
He approached and stood before Anshar.
When Anshar saw him, his heart filled with joy.
He kissed his lips and his fear departed from him
"Anshar, be not muted; open wide thy lips.
I will go and attain thy heart's desire.
Anshar, be not muted; open wide your lips.
I will go and attain your heart's desire!
What male is it who has pressed his fight against you?

Tiamat, a woman that flies at you with weapons!
begetter of the gods, be glad and rejoice;
You shall soon tread upon the neck of Tiamat!
... Anshar, my father, be glad and rejoice;
You shall soon tread upon the neck of Tiamat!"

"My son, you who knows all wisdom,
Calm Tiamat with your holy spell.

"*If she will not listen to your word, Then tell her our word, that she might be calmed.*" If Tiamat is not calmed by the words of Ea, then we have no choice but repeating what was already said: "*I will destroy, wreak their ways.*" Yet when Ea approached Tiamat, there was no fight in him. Here, as we said, the tablet is altered and illegible. But a segment discovered recently deciphered by Zecharia Sitchin in his book *The Twelfth Planet*, seems more fitting to begin Tablet III than on the next page :

Tablet 3

In the chamber of fates, the abode of destinies,
A god was engendered, most able and wisest of gods.
In the heart of the abyss was Marduk created;
In the heart of holy deep was Marduk created.

Alluring was his figure, sparkling the lift of his eyes,
Lordly was his gait, commanding from of old,
Surpassing all gods, exceeding tall.

A new god of heaven, that is, another planet, joines the drama after being formed in deep space where destinies, that is, the positions and orbits of planets are set. In Sumerian cuneiform texts it is named "Nibiru," a planet projected into space, and then trapped by the solar system's gravity and moved inside it, in the opposite direction and at a right angle to the solar system plane. As we shall see later on, its course makes it collide with Tiamat.

The narrative of the later, Babylonian version was modified to "humor" Marduk, the chief deity of Babylon, also called Bel-Merodach, and who is referred to in the Bible as "Lord." From now on, planet Nibiru is renamed **Marduk**.

Being the twelfth solar system body, Marduk appears ahead of the eleventh planet which was about to appear right away. The emergence of Marduk offers an opportunity to resolve the situation Ea has gotten into with Anshar and his fellows. Thus Ea, addressing Marduk, tells him: "*My son Marduk… approach as though in combat.*"

"*The lord rejoiced at the word of his father,*" so Marduk hurries up to Anshar. After exchanging some pleasantries and words of encouragement, Marduk undertakes the assignment, and Anshar, flattering him, bids:

"Calm Tiamat with your holy spell.

Go with all speed to Tiamat
Once she sees you, she is bound to flee."

His heart exulting, he said to his father:
"Creator of the gods, destiny of the great gods,
If I indeed, as your avenger,
Conquer Tiamat and give you life,
Set up the Assembly, proclaim my destiny to be supreme!
When jointly in Ubshukinnak you have sat down rejoicing,
Let my word, instead of you, determine the fates.
What I may bring into being shall be unalterable;
The command of my lips shall be neither recalled nor changed."

Tablet III:

Anshar opened his mouth and
Addressed a word to Gaga, his minister:
"O Gaga, my vizier, who gladdens my spirit,
I will dispatch you to Lahmu and Lahamu.

Tell them my heart's desire
Haste to assemble the Gods of Heaven
Let them hold converse, sit down to a banquet,
Let them eat bread, let them mix wine,
For Marduk, their avenger, let them fix the decrees.

Marduk's response to the biddings is "***Set up the Assembly, proclaim my destiny to be supreme!***" That is, he insists that the orbit allotted to him as his reward for vanquishing Tiamat is the most significant in the solar system. And indeed, the course of Nibiru/Marduk approaches that of the other planets until it is trapped by the strong gravity of the two largest planets, Anshar and Kishar. As a result, it is deflected towards the solar system, crossing it, revolving around the Sun and then, in an elongated elliptic orbit, goes back into deep space. From that distant point, it starts another revolution around the Sun, periodically (see Illustration 5). Such a phenomenon of a planet repulsed by an explosion into space and then trapped by solar system gravity had already been observed by astronomers and astrophysicists. According to astronomers, this is how the regular orbit of a planet trapped by another solar system's gravity is formed.

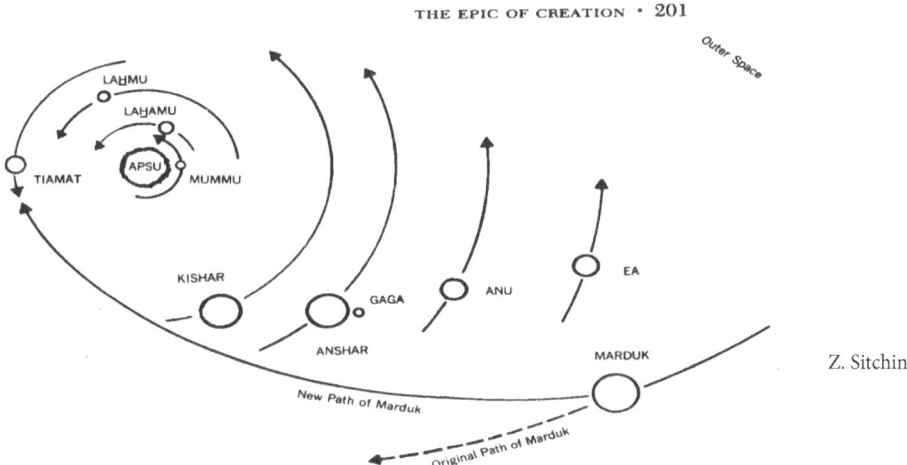

Illustration 5: Pluto, Gaga, the newest of planets, has changed its positon since then, and is now behind Neptune/Nudimmud

"***Anshar opened his mouth and addressed a word to Gaga, his minister***": Though in the original text, this is beginning of Tablet III, yet the contents is the sequel of the previous text. Gaga is Pluto, the eleventh planet of the system. In the Sumerian texts, Gaga traveled near Anshar, initially, and was regarded Anshar's minister. Therefore, he is told to convene all Gods of Heaven and their hosts:

Be on your way, Gaga, take the stand before them,
And that which I shall tell you repeat to them:
'Anshar, your son, has sent me here,
Charging me to give voice to the dictates of his heart,
He says that Tiamat, she who bore us, detests us.
She has set up the Assembly and is furious with rage.
All the gods have rallied to her;
Even those whom you brought forth march at her side.
They throng and march at the side of Tiamat.
Enraged, they plot without cease night and day.

They are set for combat, growling, raging,
They have formed a council to prepare for the fight.
Mother Hubur, she who fashions all things,
Has added matchless weapons, has born monster-serpents,
Sharp of tooth, unsparing of fang.
With venom for blood she has filled their bodies.
Roaring dragons she has clothed with terror,
Has crowned them with haloes, making them like gods,
So that he who beholds them is overcome by terror,
Their bodies rear up and none can withstand their attack.

She has set up a Viper, a Dragon, and a monster;
A Great-Lion, a Mad-Dog, and a Scorpion-Man,
Mighty lion-demons, a Dragon-Fly, a Centaur—
Bearing weapons that spare not, fearless in battle.
Her decrees are firm, none can resist them;
After this fashion eleven of this kind she has brought forth.
She has elevated Kingu, has made him chief among them.

The leading of the ranks, command of the Assembly,
To direct the battle, to control the fight.

Anshar commands Gaga to tell give a full account of the events: "***Tiamat, she who bore us, detests us.***" This phrase is an addition of Anshar's followers, and Anshar, too, retells most meticulously Tiamat's deeds, as told him by Ea and as he retold Gaga: "***She…is furious with rage…To direct the battle***…" Anshar goes on, retelling the events for another page, and then Gaga, too, retells the events for another two pages, using the very same words.

I shall tell you repeat to them:
'Anshar, your son, has sent me here,
Charging me to give voice to the dictates of his heart,
He says that Tiamat, she who bore us, detests us.

All the gods have rallied to her;
Even those whom you brought forth march at her side.

They are set for combat, growling, raging,
They have formed a council to prepare for the fight.

She has elevated Kingu, has made him chief among them.

The leading of the ranks, command of the Assembly,
To direct the battle, to control the fight.

Epic personification aside, one may conclude that at this stage, creation is accomplished, and we have a solar system of twelve heavenly bodies, or Gods of Heaven, with the Sun at its center and ten planets orbiting around it. Another planet, Nibiru/Marduk, was trapped by the gravitational pull of the two largest planets, and had its course deflected towards the system, facing the major celestial event which would decide its destiny, as shown in Illustration 5.

From among the gods, her first-born, who formed her Assembly,
She has made him chief among them.
To direct the battle, to control the fight,
"I have cast the spell for you, exalting you in the Assembly of the gods.
To counsel all the gods I have given you full power.
Truly, you are supreme, you are my only consort!
Your utterance shall prevail over all the Anunnaki!"
She has given him the Tablet of Destinies, fastened on his breast;
"As for you, your command shall be unchangeable, your word shall endure!".
As soon as Kingu was elevated, possessed of the rank of Anu,
For the gods, her sons, they decreed the fate.

"Your word shall make the fire subside,
Shall humble the "Power-Weapon," so potent in its sweep!."
I sent forth Anu; he could not face her.
Nudimmud was afraid and turned back.
But Marduk came forth, the wisest of gods, your son,
His heart having prompted him to set out to face Tiamat.
He opened his mouth, saying unto me:
"If I indeed, as your avenger,
Am to vanquish Tiamat and save your lives,
Set up the Assembly, proclaim supreme my destiny!
When jointly in Ubshukinnak you sit down rejoicing,
Let my word, instead of you, determine the fates.

Unalterable shall be what I may bring into being;
Neither recalled nor changed shall be the command of my lips!"
Now hasten here and promptly fix for him your decrees,
That he may go forth to face your mighty foe!"
Gaga departed, proceeding on his way.
Before Lahmu and Lahamu, the gods, his fathers,
He made obeisance, kissing the ground at their feet.
He bowed low as he took his place to address them:

"*She has made him chief among them*," refers, naturally, to Kingu. Here Anshar's retelling ends, with words of his own: "*I sent forth Anu…; Ea was afraid….*" Then Marduk, the wisest of the gods, rose "*…jointly in Ubshukinnak you sit down rejoicing*" So Anshar concludes, stating: "*Now hasten here and promptly fix for him your decrees, That he may go forth to face your mighty foe…*"

Now Gaga, or Pluto, the last planet, is to undertake the assignment of Anshar, so "*He took his place to address them*," retelling once again the story for another two pages, this time to Lahmu and Lahamu. With additions of his own, to enhance the plot: "*Anshar, your son, sent me…*"

The state of affairs at this stage confirms our interpretation of the epic: the eleven heavenly bodies, namely the Sun, the Moon and another nine planets, are expecting Marduk, the twelfth planet. Thus, the Sumerian/Akkadian narrative introduces us to the accelerated course of Marduk past Nudimmud/Ea/Neptune and Anu/Uranus, approaching Anshar/Saturn. Then its course starts to deflect until, when passing by Kishar/Jupiter, the largest planet of the solar system, which has a powerful gravity, is already deflected and set on a collision course with Tiamat.

The existence of an ancient planet discovered on the edge of the solar system by the Hubble Space Telescope (see Picture A). This planet named **Methuselah**, alongside Apsu/Sun and Kingu/Moon, makes the solar system count twelve, corresponding to the number of Sumerian Pantheon of gods.

Yet the ancients had already known about Nibiru/Marduk millennia ago, and in many Sumerian and Akkadian texts it was referred to as the planet of the Nephilim, as shall be explained later on. In a later period, it came to be symbolized by a winged globe.

Illustration 6

Your son Anshar sent me to tell you the wish of his heart:
Tiamat, she who bore us, detests us.
She has set up the Assembly and is furious with rage.
All the gods have rallied to her;
Even those whom you brought forth march at her side.
They throng and march at the side of Tiamat.
Enraged, they plot without cease night and day.
They are set for combat, growling, raging,
They have formed a council to prepare for the fight.

Mother Hubur, she who fashions all things,
Has added matchless weapons, has born monster-serpents,

Sharp of tooth, unsparing of fang.
With venom for blood she has filled their bodies.
Roaring dragons she has clothed with terror,
Has crowned them with haloes, making them like gods,
So that he who beholds them is overcome by terror,
Their bodies rear up and none can withstand their attack.

She has set up a Viper, a Dragon, and a monster Lahamu,
A Great-Lion, a Mad-Dog, and a Scorpion-Man,
Mighty lion-demons, a Dragon-Fly, a Centaur—
Bearing weapons that spare not, fearless in battle.
Her decrees are firm, none can resist them;
After this fashion eleven of this kind she has brought forth.
From among the gods, her first-born, who formed her Assembly,
She has elevated Kingu, has made him chief among them.
The leading of the ranks, command of the Assembly,
The raising of weapons for the encounter, advancing to combat,
To direct the battle, to control the fight,

In 1977, NASA had launched two space probes, Voyager 1 and Voyager 2. A few years later, Voyager 1 has sent signals from beyond the farthest planets of the solar system, and in 1987, the world press reported the existence of another solar system planet.

מדע / מיכאל גרטי

2.7.1987 "הארץ"

כוכב הלכת העשירי

מקור העדויות לקיומו של כוכב לכת נוסף במערכת השמש ב־100 שנות תצפית • מאז 1910 לא נמצאו כל עדויות נוספות • אם אכן קיימת פלנטה עשירית – מסתה גדולה פי 5 ממסת הארץ והיא מקיפה את השמש אחת ל־700 שנה במסלול אליפטי מרוחק

עדויות המצביעות על קיום אפשרי של כוכב לכת עשירי במערכת השמש נבחנו על־ידי אסטרונומים בארה"ב, ומהן עולה כי אם אכן קיימת פלנטה עשירית, מגיעה מסתה לחמש מסות ארץ, ומסלולה אליפטי ומוטה כמעט בזווית ישרה לעומת מסלוליהם של שאר כוכבי הלכת. משך ההקפה של הפלנטה עשירית סביב השמש מגיע ל־700 שנה.

ג'ון אנדרסון, מדען בסוכנות החלל האמריקאית (נאס"א), אמר לאחרונה כי חלק מהעדויות שהוביל למסקנה שכוכב לכת עשירי אכן קיים בשוליים הרחוקים של מערכת השמש, מבוסס על תצפיות שנעשו מתחילת המאה ה־19 ועד 1910 – שהעלו שינויים במסלוליהם של כוכבי הלכת אורנוס ונפטון, הפלנטות השביעית והשמינית של מערכת השמש.

השפעתה של פלנטה עשירית, מרוחקת יותר, יכולה להסביר את הסטיות במסלולי אורנוס ונפטון – אך הבעיה בקבלת פירוש זה נובעת מכך שלמרות שסטיות אלו ניצפו במשך 100 שנה, שמאז 1910 לא היו שינויים בתנועתן של שתי פלנטות אלו, שאינם מוסברים גם ללא הימצאות פלנטה עשירית.

לדברי אנדרסון, אין גם כל עדות להשפעה גרוויטציונית של פלנטה חיצונית על מסלוליהן של שתי חלליות פיוניר (10 ו־11) ששוגרו לפני 15 שנה, ועדיין נעות בשולי מערכת השמש. חלליות אלו – ששוגרו לחקר יופיטר – רגישות אפילו לשינויים הקלים ביותר בשדה הכובד.

עד שנת 2500

אם אכן מדוייקות המדידות שהביאו במשך כמאה שנה לתוצאות עקביות באשר למסלולי אורנוס ונפטון – מדוע אין הפלנטה ה־10 משפיעה על פלנטות אלו, ועל חלליות הפיוניר, גם עכשיו?

התשובה נקוצה ככל הנראה במסלולו של כוכב הלכת העשירי. המסלול, כפי שאפשר להסיק מניתוח נתוני התצפיות במאה ה־19, הוא כה מרוחק, ומשך ההקפה נע בין 700 ל־1,000 שנה – כך שהשפעתו לא תהיה ניכרת לפחות עד לשנת 2500.

"כדי להסביר מה גרם לסטיות במסלולי אורנוס ונפטון במשך יותר מ־100 שנה", אומר אנדרסון, "עלינו ליצור פלנטה x, כאשר מחברים יחד את כל הנתונים מגיעים לתסריט שלפיו פלנטה x היא הגורמת להפרעות".

קיומו של כוכב לכת עשירי הוא לדעת אסטרונומים רבים הגורם העיקרי למחזורים של התנגשויות כוכבי שביט בכדור הארץ. התיאוריה הנוגעת למחזורי השביטים מכנה לעיתים את הפלנטה העשירית בשם "כוכב המוות" – כוכב המתקרב אחת לפרקי זמן ארוכים (בהשפעת כבידה של כוכבי הלכת האחרים המסיטה אותו ממסלולו) אל מעטפת אורט: מעטפת של גושי קרח המצוייה הרחק בשולי מערכת השמש, ובהשפעת כוח הכובד שלו מוסטים גושים אלה ממסלולם, והופכים לכוכבי שביט שחלקם פוגעים בכדור הארץ.

השם "כוכב המוות" ניתן לפלנטה זו, כיוון שמשערים כי מבחי השביטים הם שגרמו להכחדה מחזורית של בעלי־חיים על פני כדור הארץ – הכחדה שעקבותיה הגיאולוגיים מעידים על מחזוריות של אחת ל־26 מיליון שנה, כשהפגיעה המוכרת ביותר היא זו שהביאה להכחדת הדינוזאורים לפני 65 מיליון שנה.

המסלול המוטה ב־90 מעלות למסלוליהם של שאר כוכבי הלכת, ובעל צורה אליפטית הזה, אינו יוצא דופן במערכת השמש – שכן גם לפלוטו, כוכב הלכת התשיעי, מסלול אליפטי מאוד הנוטה ב־30 מעלות לעומת מסלוליהם של שאר כוכבי הלכת – וכן מציינים האסטרונומים את טריטון – הירח הענק של נפטון, שמסלולו נוטה לעומת מישור שאר המסלולים, וכיוון ההקפה שלו סביב הפלנטה הפוך מכיווניהם של שאר הירחים במערכת השמש.

על־פי חישובי המסלול האפשריים, פלנטה x – אם היא אכן קיימת – חלפה בנקודה הקרובה ביותר לשמש במסלולה בשנת 1750 ותשוב אליה ב־2800. אך לדברי מדעני נאסא, אין פירוש הדבר שנצטרך להמתין עד שנת 2500 לפני שאפשר יהיה לאמת את היצאותו או העדרותו של כוכב הלכת העשירי. ציוד מדידה רגיש בחלליות שישוגרו בעתיד יוכל לענות על השאלה אולי עוד לפני סוף המאה ה־20.

כוכב הלכת ניבירו/מרדוך הוא השנים-עשר במספר. על פי פירסום זה, כוכב הלכת מקיף את השמש אחת ל-700 שנה. במקרא יש רמזים שתקופה זו ארוכה יותר, שלא להזכיר טקסטים מסופוטמים העוסקים בנושא והם מצביעים על כך שזמן הקפתו של ניבירו את השמש הוא ממושך יותר. בספרו The Twelfth Planet, מגיע זכריה סיטשין למסקנה שהקפה אחת נמשכת תקופת זמן של 3,600 שנים. נושא זה ידון בפירוט יותר בפרק הבא על הנפילים.

האפוס אנומה-עליש היה נחשב למקודש בשומר העתיקה והיה נקרא במקדשים בראש השנה החדשה. הכוהן הגדול היה יוצא לרחבה שלפני המקדש, מרים ראשו אל על וצופה בשמים על מנת לזהות את כוכב הלכת הזוהר.

Picture 3: Israeli daily *Haaretz* reports on the 2.7.1987. The discovery of the tenth planet

I have cast the spell for you, exalting you in the Assembly of the gods.
To counsel all the gods I have given you full power.
Truly, you are supreme, you are my only consort!
Your utterance shall prevail over all the Anunnaki!"
She has given him the Tablet of Destinies, fastened on his breast:
"As for you, your command shall be unchangeable, your word shall endure!"
As soon as Kingu was elevated, possessed of the rank of Anu,
For the gods, her sons, they decreed the fate:
"Your word shall make the fire subside,
Shall humble the "Power-Weapon," so potent in its sweep!"

I sent forth Anu; he could not face her.
Nudimmud was afraid and turned back.
But Marduk came forth, the wisest of gods, your son,
His heart having prompted him to set out to face Tiamat.
He opened his mouth, saying unto me:
"If I indeed, as your avenger,
Am to vanquish Tiamat and save your lives,
Set up the Assembly, proclaim supreme my destiny!
When in Ubshukinnak jointly you sit down rejoicing,
Let my word, instead of you, determine the fates.

Unalterable shall be what I may bring into being;
Neither recalled nor changed shall be the command of my lips!"
Now hasten here and promptly fix for him your decrees,
That he may go forth to face your mighty foe!"
When Lahmu and Lahamu heard this, they cried out aloud,
All the Igigi wailed in distress:
'How strange that she should have made this decision!
We cannot fathom the doings of Tiamat!'

Approaching Lahamu and Lahmu, and reporting to them all the deeds of Tiamat, Gaga added that Marduk, the wisest of gods, volunteered to face Tiamat single handedly, and, indeed, *opened his mouth, saying:* "***If I indeed….Am to vanquish Tiamat and save your lives….Set up the Assembly, proclaim supreme my destiny!***" Gaga concludes, stating, "***Now hasten here and promptly fix for him his decrees.***"

The news of what Gaga had told Lahmu and Lahamu about Marduk reached others, including the "***all the Igigi***," who wailed in distress. The Igigi are not part of the Gods of Heaven, and this is the first time the epic mentions entities other than Gods of Heaven, that is, solar system bodies. Rather than Gods of Heaven, the Igigi are "sons of gods," or Gods of Heaven and Earth. In other words, they are the gods who didn't descend from their spacecraft to Earth as the words of the Bible, in *Psalms* 69:18-19 describe: "**C*hariots of God ribotaim (a big mass of 20,000,) Thousands of escorts, Jehovah (the Lord) is with them, Sinai in holy.***" This means: the Lord came down from heaven to Earth in a chariot, descending on Sinai, where the Revelation took place. Jehovah, the Lord of Heaven and Earth, is the name of both the lord of Enuma Elish and that of the Bible, since Enuma Elish, being older than the Bible, served as the source, background and inspiration of biblical narratives. Another hint to the God shared by both creation stories is in *Genesis* 6:4: "…***and the Nephilim were on Earth, that the sons of God came in unto the daughters of men.***" The Igigi were part of those sons of God. But this calls for a much more elaborated explanation, presented further on. Here, one should also compare the two creation stories from another aspect, namely the concept of deity. This is one of the major differences between the biblical and Mesopotamian creation narratives. This is evident at the beginning of the biblical version where it the name of God is mentioned: "In the beginning, **God** Created Heaven and Earth"; "*the Spirit of **God** moved…*"; and, at the very same chapter, "**God** saw," "**God** made… and divided"; "**God** called…"; God said….." Throughout, God's name recurs nearly another twenty-eight times until the end of Chapter 1. Unlike it, the first time god is mentioned in the Enuma Elish is no sooner than line 7: ***None of the gods had been brought into being And none bore a name.***…and, a line later, "***Then it was that the gods were formed in the midst of heaven.***" In addition, these gods, unlike the biblical God, are Gods of Heaven, the Mesopotamian epithet of the solar system's heavenly bodies. In this sense the Sumerian cosmogony is more elaborate, and, being unaffected by any religious doctrine, it offers a sophisticated representation of the cosmos, acceptable to scientists. Moreover, while the biblical narrative suggests that God created the world by his words, according to Enuma Elish, it was Apsu, the Sun, who was "***The primordial, creator of all.***"

They made ready to leave on their journey,
All the great gods who decree the fates.
They entered before Anshar, filling Ubshukinnak.
They kissed one another in the Assembly.
They held converse as they sat down to the banquet.
They ate bread, they mixed wine.
They wetted their drinking-tubes with sweet intoxicant.
As they drank the strong drink, their bodies swelled.
They became very languid as their spirits rose.
For Marduk, their avenger, they fixed the decrees.

[Tablet IV]

They erected for him a princely throne.

Facing his fathers, he sat down, presiding.
"You are the most honored of the great gods,
Your decree is unrivaled, your word is Anu.
You, Marduk, are the most honored of the great gods,
Your decree is unrivaled, your command is Anu.
From this day your pronouncement shall be unchangeable.
To raise or bring low—these shall be in your hand.
Your utterance shall be true, your command shall be unimpeachable.

O Marduk, you are indeed our avenger.

We have granted you kingship over the universe entire.
When you sit in Assembly your word shall be supreme.
Your weapons shall not fail; they shall smash your foes!
O lord, spare the life of him who trusts you,
But pour out the life of the god who seized evil."

As all the great gods, filling the Ubshukinnak, or Assembly Hall, "***They wetted their drinking-tubes with sweet intoxicant.***" This concluding statement is rather cynical, since they not only had "**sweet intoxicant**," but also became full and drunk, "***as their spirits rose. For Marduk, their avenger, they fixed the decrees.***" Just like that, with no deliberation or reflection, they decided to allot to Marduk the longest orbit around the Sun.

Although everything said so far was just to prepare the exultation of Marduk as presented in Tablet IV, but it may also indicate to the attitude towards other gods.

Tablet IV

They erected for him a princely throne.

Facing his fathers, he sat down, presiding.

This segment and the following are translated from the late Babylonian version, since recent researchers disagree on the accurate dating of this epic. However, looking at its contents and language, most scholars date it to early Babylonian period, that is, the first half of second millennium B.C.E. As we said, the Babylonian version was modified and phrases were added which present Marduk as chief Babylonian deity and portray the Celestial Battle as a metaphor of the triumphant battle of Marduk with other members of the Sumerian Pantheon, for the position of chief and only deity during his reign on Earth. This is stressed in the phrases referring to the god's name:

Thy decree is unrivaled, your command is Anu.

And two lines later: **"thy decree is unrivaled, thy words is Anu"**

Anu was the chief of the Sumerian Pantheon, father of the gods and a supreme ruler dwelling in heavens, on Nibiru. Assigning this power to Marduk, equaling him to Anu, attests to the high position of Marduk as the chief Babylonian deity in the second millennium B.C.E.

"May thy fate, O lord, be supreme among the gods,
Say but to wreck or create; it shall be.
Open your mouth: the garment will vanish!
Speak again, and the garment shall be whole!"
At the word of his mouth the garment vanished.
He spoke again, and the garment was restored.
When the gods, his fathers, saw the fruit of his word,
Joyfully they did homage: "Marduk is king!"
They conferred on him scepter, throne, and vestment;
They gave him matchless weapons that ward off the foe.
"Go and cut off the life of Tiamat.
May the winds bear her blood to places undisclosed."
Bel's - (Marduk) destiny thus fixed, the gods, his fathers,
Caused him to go the way of success and attainment.
He constructed a bow, marked it as his weapon,
Attached thereto the arrow, fixed its bow-cord.
He raised the mace, made his right hand grasp it;
Bow and quiver he hung at his side.
In front of him he set the lightning,
With a blazing flame he filled his body.

He then made nets to enfold Tiamat therein.
The four winds he stationed that nothing of her might escape,
from South and North, East and West.
Close to his side he held the net, a gift of his father Anu.
He created Bad wind, Evil wind, whirlwind and cyclone.

When the words and commands of Marduk are compared with those of Anu, the author endows him with powers and authority no other member of the Pantheon had enjoyed. In some translations such as the Hebrew one, the name of Anu is not mentioned in this segment. Probably, the author disapproved of the Position of Anu as chief deity, since, for instance, Anu is said to lose heart when facing Tiamat: "*I sent forth Anu; he could not face her.*" (Tablet III – page 42?)

"*Open your mouth: the garment will vanish*":

This magic scene was very common in ancient literature, and it certainly brings to mind the magic feats Moses had performed to impress the pharaoh and his court such as transforming a stick into snake, beating water out of a desert rock, and many other supernatural events by which prophets or judges demonstrated their powers to their audience.

The gods, having witnessed and being strongly impressed by Marduk's capability, urge him: "**Go and cut off… the life of Tiamat**." So he loses no time: "**He constructed a bow… Attached thereto the arrow, raised the mace**," and carried out other actions which can be read as metaphors for cosmic phenomena resulting from planets getting too close to each other. The net made to enfold Tiamat is the gravitational force of Marduk, while the four winds he created are four satellites, out of the many satellites of Anu, or Uranus, Marduk had attracted when approaching the solar system: "**the gift of his father, Anu: Bad wind, Evil wind, Whirlwind, Cyclone**."

Looking at Illustration 4, we can clearly see that Marduk is already past Pluto, approaching Anshar and Gaga; his nearby minister, Gaga, or Pluto, as we know it today, is the farthest planet, situated far beyond Nudimmud, or Neptune. Other texts on this subject reveal that Gaga was repelled by Marduk and in the course of time assumed its position behind Nudimmud as the farthest planet.

Later on in its journey, Marduk came closer to Kishar, or Jupiter, a large planet of the greatest gravitational force. The illustration shows that the course of Marduk was deflected towards the solar system, and was bound to collide with Tiamat.

Then he sent forth the seven winds he had brought forth,
To stir up the inside of Tiamat they rose up behind him.
Then the lord raised up the flood-storm, his mighty weapon.
He mounted the storm-chariot irresistible and terrifying.

He harnessed and yoked to it a team-of-four,

A Killer, a Relentless, a Trampler and a Swift.
Their lips were parted, their teeth bore poison.
They were tireless and skilled in destruction.
On his right he posted the Smiter, fearsome in battle,
On the left the Combat, which repels all the zealous.
For a cloak he was wrapped in an armor of terror;
With his fearsome halo his head was turbaned.
The lord went forth and followed his course,
Towards the raging Tiamat he set his face.

In his lips he held a spell;
A plant to put out poison was grasped in his hand.
Then they milled about him, the gods milled about him,
The gods, his fathers milled about him, they milled about him.
The lord approached to scan the inside of Tiamat,
And of Kingu, her consort, the scheme to perceive.
As he looks on, he loses his way,
His will is distracted and his doings are confused.
And when the gods, his helpers, who marched at his side,
Saw the valiant hero, their vision became blurred.

Tiamat emitted a cry, her neck she turned not.
Words of cruel defiance in her lip extended:
"Have you become the lord of the gods?
Or did you make their place your own?"

"*The winds he had brought forth, ... To stir up the inside of Tiamat,*" are the four "winds," or satellites it had attracted from Anu, or Uranus, and another three it had earlier, which he sent forth to unnerve Tiamat. Before the actual battle starts, Marduk makes many attempts of intimidation, greatly impressing the gods, especially Kingu: "*As he looks on, he loses his way.*"

Yet Tiamat was not scared, and, "**without turning her neck**," leveled at Marduk a string of curses and poignant defiant statements: "**Have you become the lord of the gods? Or did you make their place your own?**"

In the original, these lines are unclear. A plausible translation, using several English translations, may read:

Tiamat emitted (a shout), her neck she turned not,

Words of cruel defiance her lips extended:

Too beloved art thou (...) the lord of gods to rise against;

Have they gathered in their place (...) in thy place?

The Hebrew translation reads, "**Have you become the lord of gods? Or did you make their place your own**?"

Despite all the epic personification and animation of heavenly bodies, what we can see here is a description of a cosmic event in the distant past that formed the solar system and human lives on Earth. A large, ancient planet, with a volume nearly five times that of Earth, was repulsed into space as a result of the explosion of the star it had previously revolved around, namely the Sun. That planet, Nibiru/Marduk, traveling through the cosmos, approached the fledgling solar system at right angle to its plane and in a direction opposite to its planets revolution- that is, counterclockwise. When passing by the outer planets, its course was deflected inside the planet and was set on a collision course with Tiamat. At this stage, the collision is yet to take place, but the epic has already depicts several actions introducing the collision: Marduk had brought forth seven winds and yoked a team of four; Kingu loses his way; Tiamat utters cruel defiance, etc.

All these are psychological warfare tactics, solely intended to unnerve the opponent, but are not enough to subdue him completely and decide the battle. As part of these intimidating maneuvers, some altercations take place between the rivals, for tactical purposes, as a preparation for taking more drastic measures:

Thereupon the lord, having raised the flood-storm, his mighty weapon,
To enraged Tiamat he sent word as follows:
"Why are you risen, haughtily exalted,
You have charged your own heart **to stir up conflict,**... sons reject their own fathers,
While you, who have born them, have foresworn love!

You have appointed Kingu as your consort,
Conferring upon him the rank of Anu, not rightfully his.
Against Anshar, king of the gods, you seek evil;
Against the gods, my fathers, you have confirmed your wickedness.
Though your forces are drawn up, your weapons girded on,
Stand up, that I and you might meet in single combat!"
When Tiamat heard this, She was like one possessed;
She took leave of her senses.
In fury Tiamat cried out aloud.
To the roots her legs shook both together.

She recites a charm, keeps casting her spell,
While the gods of battle sharpen their weapons.
Then Tiamat and Marduk joined issue, wisest of gods.
They strove in single combat, locked in battle.
The lord spread out his net to enfold her,
The Evil Wind, which followed behind, he let loose in her face.
When Tiamat opened her mouth to consume him,
He drove in the Evil Wind while as yet she had not shut her lips
As the terrible winds filled her belly,
Her body was distended and her mouth was wide open.
He released the arrow, it tore her belly,
It cut through her insides, splitting the heart.

"*Thereupon the lord, having raised the flood-storm,*" refers to one of the winds, or satellites, drawn from Anu/Uranus when passing near it. This is when the Celestial Battle actually begins, when the flood-storm hits Tiamat. It is followed by an exchange of defiance and scorning which infuriated Tiamat, and eventually, drove the two rivals to clash: "*They strove in single combat, locked in battle.*"

Some earlier translators failed to understand the significance of Anu as the chief Sumerian deity and the ancestor of the Sumerian Pantheon, which is stressed in all Mesopotamian texts. Its top position was unquestionable, being the founder of a ruling godly dynasty, succeeded by his sons, Enlil and Enki/Ea, who followed him from heaven, as well as their relatives and decedents born on Earth. Kingu, also known as Nanar/Sin, was the son of Enlil, while Marduk was the son of Enki. These two cousins, and their families, fought over regional domination, and the epic compares their power struggle to the Celestial Battle, where Anu's preeminence is fully stressed:

"*Thou hast appointed Kingu as thy consort, Conferring upon him the rank of Anu, not rightfully his.*" Here, too, the empowerment of Kingu is a major defiance of Marduk's status as chief Babylonian deity in the late second millennium B.C.E. By this statement, Marduk betrays his feeling of being discriminated against, in favor of Kingu/Sin.

"*The lord spread out his net to enfold her, The Evil Wind, which followed behind, he let loose in her face*": The net refers to the effects of Marduk's gravitational forces while the Evil Wind is just another of the four satellites Marduk had attracted away from Anu while approaching the system's planets. "*The arrow*" released is lightning that resulted from voltage differences between large heavenly bodies.

Having thus subdued her, he depressed her life.
He cast down her carcass to stand upon it.
After he had slain Tiamat, the leader,
Her band was shattered, her troop broken up;
And the gods, her helpers who marched at her side,
Trembling with terror, turned their backs about,
In order to save and preserve their lives.
Tightly encircled, they could not escape.

He made them captives and he smashed their weapons.
Thrown into the net, they found themselves ensnared;
Placed in cells, they were filled with wailing;
Bearing his wrath, they were held imprisoned.
And the eleven creatures which she had charged with awe,
The whole band of demons that marched on her right,
He cast into fetters, their hands he bound.
For all their resistance, he trampled them underfoot.
And Kingu, who had been made chief among them,
He submissed and Bound to Uggae.

He took from him the Tablet of Destinies, not rightfully his,
Sealed them with a seal and fastened them on his breast.
When he had vanquished and subdued his adversaries,
Had... the vain glorious foe,
Had wholly established Anshar's triumph over the foe,
Had achieved Nudimmud's desire, valiant Marduk
Strengthened his hold on the vanquished gods,
And turned back to Tiamat whom he had bound.
The lord trod on the legs of Tiamat,
With his unsparing mace he crushed her skull.

When the arteries of her blood he had severed,
The North Wind bore it to places undisclosed.

This segment accounts for several well-known cosmic phenomena occurring when heavenly bodies get excessively close to each other while orbiting the Sun: lightning, thunderstorms, gravity and anti-gravity force effects, solid and liquid substances overflowing from one planet to another, and other phenomena discussed later on.

"*Her band…the gods…..turned their backs about….Tightly encircled.*" This may account for the phenomenon of the orbits and times of appearance near Earth being practically unpredictable. "[T]*he gods, her helpers who marched at her side*" are the smaller satellites, made of material attracted from space by Tiamat's gravitational force, orbiting it. They were repulsed but "enclosed," that is, they are still bound by the system's gravity and reappear irregularly and at unexpected orbits. "[T]*he eleven creatures which she had charged with awe*," together with "**her helpers**," were cast into fetters, that is, were kept bound by the gravitational force, doomed, as comets, to orbit the Sun.

Kingu, in another version, was not "**Bound to Uggae**," that is, sacrificed to death but "*turned into Duggae*," that is, a lead pot. In other words, Kingu, the Moon was not killed but turned into an inanimate lead pot, losing the Tablets of Destinies. Thus, it was doomed to remain one of the eleven solar system bodies, and plays an important role towards the end of the epic, when he [Marduk] caused the Moon = Sin/Kingu to shine, entrusting the night to him.

Meanwhile, Marduk didn't stop at subjugating Tiamat, but "***turned back to her***," "***trod on her legs***," "***crushed her skull***" and "***severed her arteries***," so "*the North Wind bore it to places undisclosed.*" This refers to the half of Tiamat scattered where it used to revolve, as we shall see later on. Its other half, which hadn't been scattered, was repulsed to its new position between Lahmu and Lahamu, that is, Venus and Mars. What happened to its waters is also reported in *Genesis* 1:9: "***Let the waters ….be gathered together unto one place***." That is to say, the water was drained to the missing western hemisphere, where oceans are situated, while land appeared on the eastern hemisphere. Thus, Tiamat came to be planet Earth, repelled into space to its new position where it trapped Kingu, the Moon, making it its satellite.

On seeing this, his fathers were joyful and jubilant,
They brought gifts of homage to him.
Then the lord paused to view her submissive body,
That he might divide the form and do artful works.
He split her like a shellfish into two parts:
Half of her he set up as a covering for heaven,
Pulled down the bar and posted guards.
He bade them to allow not her waters to escape.

He crossed the heavens and surveyed the regions.
He squared the deep, the abode of Nudimmud,
As the lord measured the dimensions of the deep.
The Great Abode, its likeness, he fixed as Esharra,
The Great Abode, Esharra, which he made as the firmament.
Anu, Enlil, and Ea he made occupy their places.

Tablet V

He constructed stations for the great gods,
Fixing their astral likenesses as the stars of the Zodiac.
He determined the year and into sections he divided it;
He set up three constellations for each of the twelve months.
After defining the days of the year by means of heavenly figures,
He founded the station of Nibiru to determine their bounds,
That none might err or go astray.
Alongside it he set up the stations of Enlil and Ea.
Having opened up the gates on both sides,
He strengthened the locks to the left and the right.
In her belly he established the zenith.

"*[A]s a covering for heaven.*" That half is the one said to be carried by the North Wind to places undisclosed. In other words, it is the asteroid belt repulsed and scattered between Lahmu/Mars and Kishar/Jupiter, described as a pearl necklace beaten in heaven, "*to allow not her waters to escape,*" or, in *Genesis*: "**And God said, Let there be a firmament in the midst of the waters, and let it divide the waters from the waters.**" That is, divide the inner planets situated between the Sun and the asteroid belt on one hand, and the outer planets, beyond the Sun, on the other hand. Scientists, too, stressed that the asteroid belt separates two groups of planets from each other.

"***The lord measured the dimensions of the deep***" refers to Planet Earth, after the water had been gathered in the remaining half, in a gap formed on one of its sides, letting the Earth appear on the other side. Comparing to *Genesis* 1:9: "**And God called the dry land Earth; and the gathering together of the waters he called the Seas**"; this accounts for the location of continents on one side of the Earth, while the oceans are on its other side. He also constructed "*The Great Abode, Esharra,*" the temple of the god, **Ashur**.

"*Anu, Enlil, and Ea he made occupy their places.*"

Tablet V

The "***stations for the great gods***" are the twelve constellations of the zodiac, at which the axis of the Earth points, inclined as a result of the collision. "***He founded the station of Nibiriu***": Nibiru, here, is a pun, since it was the original Sumerian name of the planet before being renamed Marduk in the Babylonian version. In the solar system, Nibiru came to occupy the position of Tiamat. At this stage, the epic lists all the effects of the Celestial Battle on the solar system:

a. Tiamat, or Earth, was split in two, half getting scattered in space as a firmament, or asteroid belt, while, the other half went where the water gathered, land was revealed and it became Earth (cf. *Genesis* 1:9).

b. As a result of a collision with a large heavenly body moving in the opposite direction, the direction of the Earth's rotation was reversed, so now it is counterclockwise, as opposed to the other solar system planets. It was also repulsed to a new position between Lahamu/Venus and Lahmu/Mars, attracting Kingu/Moon by its gravitational pull, making it its satellite, thus taking away its "Tablets of Destinies," that is, its own orbit around the Sun.

The Moon he caused to shine, entrusting the night to him.
He appointed him a creature of the night to signify the days,
And marked off every month, without cease, by means of his crown.
At the month's very start, rising over the land,
You shall have luminous horns to signify six days,
On the seventh day reaching a half-crown.
So shall the fifteen-day period be like one another-two halves for each month.

When the Sun overtakes you at the base of heaven,
Diminish your crown and retrogress in light.

Tablet VI

When Marduk heard the words of the gods,
His heart prompted him to fashion artful works.
Opening his mouth, he addressed Ea
To impart the plan he had conceived in his heart:
"I will take blood and fashion bone.
I will establish a savage, 'man' shall be his name.
Truly, savage-man I will create.
He shall be charged with the service of the gods
That they might be at ease!
The ways of the gods I will artfully alter.
Though alike revered, into two groups they shall be divided."
Ea answered him, speaking a word to him
Giving him another plan for the relief of the gods.

c. The eleven satellites Tiamat had had were scattered in space, becoming comets. Confined by the solar system's gravitation and approaching the system at irregular times.
d. The axis of planet Earth inclined, making a circular movement called Earth precession.
e. "*The Moon shall cause its light to shine,*" etc., until the end of the tablet, is a precise description of the behavior of the Moon and the phenomenon related to it. As part of the new celestial order forced on Earth, Marduk commanded the Moon to illuminate the night and divide the month into days. Since Tiamat is the same as Earth, it describes how the Moon relates to Earth.
f. The sources of Life and life itself were displaced to Earth from Nibiru, an ancient planet that, as confirmed by recent discoveries, was repulsed into space from a system of a planet that had exploded. As a result of a collision with Nibiru, its atmosphere, the life evolved on it, and the origins of DNA of animals and plants, were displaced to Earth.
g. Gaga, previously positioned near Anshar, was repulsed to its current position, turning into the farthest planet, and deflected to an elliptic orbit at an angle to the solar system plane, making it change its position with respect to the solar system, when approaching Earth.

Tablet VI

"*I will establish a savage, 'man' shall be his name*": this is the later Babylonian version, totally different from the Sumerian original. In the original, Marduk, yet to be made a chief deity, is not mentioned. There are numerous and elaborate descriptions of the Creation of Man in Sumerian texts, which was decided by the Assembly of Gods, and Ea, being the chief science officer to the gods, played a major part in it, as we shall see later.

"Let but one of their brothers be handed over;
He alone shall perish that mankind may be fashioned.
Let the great gods be here in Assembly,
Let the guilty be handed over that they may endure."
Marduk summoned the great gods to Assembly;
Presiding graciously, he issued instructions.
To his utterance the gods pay heed.
The king addressed a word to the Anunnaki:
"If your former statement was true,
Now declare the truth on oath by me!
Who was it that contrived the uprising,
And made Tiamat rebel, and joined battle?
Let him be handed over who contrived the uprising.
His guilt I will make him bear. You shall dwell in peace!"
The Igigi, the great gods, replied to him,
To Lugaldimmerankia, counselor of the gods, their lord:

"It was Kingu who contrived the uprising,
And made Tiamat rebel, and joined battle."

They bound him, holding him before Ea.
They imposed on him his punishment and severed his blood vessels.
Out of his blood they fashioned mankind.
He imposed on him the service and let free the gods.

The following was a later addition to Tablet VI:

After Ea, the wise, had created mankind,
Had imposed upon them the service of the gods—
That work was beyond comprehension;
As artfully planned by Marduk, did Nudimmud create it.

"[*I*]*nto two groups they shall be divided*"; one group consists of gods called Anunnaki." "Anu" meaning "heaven," and "ki" meaning "Earth," it means those who descended from heaven, the equivalent of the biblical *Nephilim* (Hebrew for "those who fell down"). The other group is the Igigi. Now, when the Celestial Battle is over, the perpetrator must be detected and punished: "**Who was it that contrived the uprising….. His guilt I will make him bear.**"

"*The Igigi, the great gods, replied to him,*

To Lugaldimmerankia, counselor of the gods, their lord";

The Igigi are another group of Nephilim, or sons of Gods of Heaven and Earth, who did not descend from heaven. *Lugaldimmerankia:* literally means "King of Gods in Heaven and on Earth."

"*It was Kingu who contrived the uprising*"; why was he punished again, after having already been punished, when Marduk, as told in Tablet IV, "**bound him to Uggae,**" and "**took from him the Tablets of Destinies.**" "**Out of his blood they fashioned mankind**"? Was it to this purpose, that "**They bound him, holding him before Ea, severed his blood vessels**"? This is discussed later in Chapter 3, which deals with the Creation of Man. The latter part of Tablet VI was corrupted, illegible when the earliest translations were published, but, recently, several other fragments have been discovered and deciphered, offering more indications that this version was a modification of the earlier Sumerian texts dealing with the Creation of Man, in order to aggrandize Marduk.

The addition to Tablet VI deals, indeed, with Ea, also known as Nudimmud, the wise creator of man. This version is compatible with the original Sumerian texts, according to which **Ea**, being chief science officer to the gods, following a decision of the assembly of gods, created man through genetic engineering manipulation, assisted by goddess **Ninhursag**, patron of medicine. It had happened long before Marduk, his son, was made chief deity in 2024 B.C.E. Only then was the original version modified, and, as a result, not all praises are addressed to **Ea**. He just did the work, "**beyond comprehension, as artfully planned by Marduk.**"

*The Anunnaki opened their mouths
And said to Marduk, their lord:
"Now, O lord, you who have caused our deliverance,
What shall be our homage to you?*

*Let us build a shrine, his name shall be called
'Lo, a chamber for our nightly rest'; let us repose in it!
Let us build a tower, a recess for his abode!
On the day that we arrive we shall repose in it."
When Marduk heard this, Brightly glowed his features, like the day:
"Construct Babylon, whose building you have requested,
Let its brickwork be fashioned. You shall name it `The Sanctuary.'"
For one whole year they molded bricks. When the second year arrived,
They raised high the head of Esagila equaling Apsu.
Having built a stage-tower as high as Apsu,
They set up in it an abode for Marduk, Enlil, and Ea.*

*"Let us do obeisance at the mention of his name,
To his utterance let the gods give heed,
Let his command be supreme above and below!
Most exalted be the Son, our avenger;
Let his sovereignty be surpassing, having no rival.
May he shepherd the black-headed ones, his creatures.
To the end of days, without forgetting, let them acclaim his ways.*

This report of the Creation of Man is a compromise between the original Sumerian version and the modified Babylonian one. Definitely, it resulted from a bitter power struggle between members of the Pantheon in 2024 B.C.E., out of which Marduk emerged unquestionably victorious, glorified as the chief deity of Sumerian Pantheon. Only then were some verses of the creation story rewritten as praises for Marduk, including the addition of his name to that of planet Nibiru, as well as Marduk's part in the creation of man.

"*Let us build a tower….Let its brickwork be fashioned…*" compare to *Genesis*11:3-4: "*And they said one to another, Go to, let us make brick……And they said, Go to, let us build us a city and a tower, whose top may reach unto heaven; and let us make us a name, lest we be scattered abroad upon the face of the whole Earth.*"

Later on, the Anunnaki exult Marduk, deciding to build a tower reaching unto heaven to honor him. Thus, unnoticed by the reader, the epic moves from the acts of Gods of Heaven, to the Gods of Heaven and Earth and their earthly deeds in honor of Marduk. It is surprisingly similar to the biblical narrative on the Tower of Babel, though there are evident differences between them. It is about the Tower of Babel, the name of the Babylonian capital and early Babylonian Kingdom, emerging in history about 1900 B.C.E. "Babel" comes from *Bab-Ilu*, "gate of the gods" or "gate of heavens," reminiscent of a place mentioned in *Genesis* 28:11-17. In the scene of Jacob's Ladder, Jacob, on his way from Beer Sheba, reaches close to Haran at Sunset, laid down to sleep in the field. "*…and he took of the stones of that place, and put them to lean his head and laid down in that place to sleep And dreamed, and behold a ladder set up on the Earth, and the top of it reached to heaven and behold the angels of God ascending and descending on it… And Jacob awaked out of his sleep, and he said, 'Indeed* **Yahweh** *is in this place; and I knew it not. And he was afraid, and said: how dreadful is this place! This is none other but the house of God, and this is the gate of heaven.'*"

In biblical narratives, dreams always have ominous meaning: that place was situated near Haran, where Terah and his household had migrated from Ur. Haran was known to be an Ur-style religious center, also called "Farther Ur."

Tablet VII is the exultation of Marduk. Now, after the work is done, he can rest, similar to the seventh day of biblical creation story. Here are highlights from that eulogy:

Truly, he is supreme in the Assembly of the gods;
None among the gods is his equal.
Established for the gods the holy heavens;
Who keeps a hold on their ways, determines their courses;
Deeds endure, not to be forgotten.

This is where the creation narrative of Sumer, the biblical Shinar, ends. As its Hebrew translator, Shaul Tchernichovsky, put it: "[T]**he war of Light and Darkness, Fall and Spring, Tiamat and Marduk, will never return again**."

The following is a juxtaposition of the concluding verses of the two creation myths:

Genesis 2:1-3

"*Thus the heavens and the Earth were finished, with all their host. And on the seventh day God finished is work which he had made; And he rested on the seventh day of all his work which he had done.. And God blessed the seventh day, and sanctified it; because he had rested that day of all his work which God created and made.*"

Enuma Elish:

He is the vessel of the stars, which shineth in the heavens.
He holds the Beginning and the Future, may they pay homage unto him,
Saying, "He who forced his way through the midst of Tiamat without resting,"
Let his name be Nibiru, 'the Seizer of the Midst'!
For the stars of heaven he upheld the paths.

CHAPTER 3

THE CREATION OF MAN

What was Lord Yahweh thinking when He decided to create Man? Did He consult his fellow gods about it? Did He envision any future function or vocation for mankind? What had He made man for, if, in *Genesis* 6:6, He already had second thoughts: "***And it repented the LORD that he had made man on the Earth, and it grieved him at his heart.***" Could Lord Yahweh have failed to foresee that near future, that he would regret having created man? These questions shall be discussed later.

According to the earliest texts dealing with the creation of man, dating back millennia before the written version of the Bible, the gods had made several failed cloning experiments. After sharing their plan with Enki, the chief scientist to the gods, they concluded that it takes mixing the male element, or *XY* chromosome, with the female element, or *XX* chromosome, to endow their new creature with reproductive capacity. Ancient Near Eastern texts frequently mention the use of a common local material, clay, serving as the earthly component, mixed with gods blood, serving as the extraterrestrial component, to create a prototype of man. The Hebrew word for clay, *tit,* is reminiscent of the word *ti-it*, or "seed of life," in Sumerian. So, when god Enki was asked to create a work of great wisdom, he found a way to design a "***servant of the gods.***" Thus, he told the mother goddess in charge of medicine:

*"Mix to a core the clay
From the Basement of Earth, just above the Abzu—
And shape it into the form of a core.*

I will prepare a purifying bath".

One of the gods will bleed…

From his flesh and blood, let Ninti mix the clay.

And what it will be is 'Man'."

And *in Genesis 1:26-27:*

And God said, Let us make man in our image, after our likeness: and let them have dominion over the fish of the sea, and over the fowl of the air, and over the cattle, and over all the Earth, and over every creeping thing that creepeth upon the Earth. So God created man in his own image, in the image of God created he him; male and female created he them.

And the LORD God formed man of the dust of the ground, and breathed into his nostrils the breath of life; and man became a living soul.

So what was that clay, the earthly ingredient used for creating man? The gods, no doubt, well acquainted with genetics, sampled an egg out of a female primate fertilized with their own sperm, implanting it in one of their daughters. Her nine-month pregnancy bore a new creature on earth, on a new evolutionary stage. The gods called it *lulu-amalu,* or "labor baby," designed to relieve the Nephilim of all hard work. Thus, the ongoing battle between evolutionists and creationists is finally resolved. Mankind is a product of evolution, upgraded thanks to a genetic engineering of the gods, he is capable of planning and being conscious of his surroundings, capable of carrying out his tasks, thanks to the capacity of learning to use his organs and senses, a capacity he received through the genes of the gods. The gods also knew how to separate the female *XX* chromosome from the male *XY* chromosome, determining an infant's gender. So, they assigned seven of their daughters to bear males, and another seven to bear females in order to hasten the production of workers of all trades required by the gods. The inevitable consequence of shared genes and physiognomic compatibility of gods and humans is reported in *Genesis* 6:

And it came to pass, when men began to multiply on the face of the Earth, And daughters were born unto them,

That the sons of God saw the daughters of men that they were fair; and they took them wives of all which they chose. (Genesis 6:1-2)

The Nephilim were on Earth in those days; and also after that, when, the sons of God came in unto the daughters of men, and they bore them children. Those were the mighty from the world, people of the SHEM. —6:4.

"*From the world,*" or "*from the universe,*" that is, from space. "**People of the SHEM**" the Akkadian word for spacecraft. No doubt the Bible deals here with extraterrestrial entities. A similar Hebrew expression, as part of reference to divine vehicles, is mentioned in *Psalms* 68:18: **The chariot of God is twenty thousand, the Lord is among them, as in Sinai, in the holy place.** Definitely, twenty thousand was an enormous amount in those days, designed to carry the thousands of *shinan,* God's escorts on his comings and goings.

For hundreds of thousands of years, since its creation until the great Flood on Earth, about 13000 years ago, human life was intertwined with that of the Nephilim in every way. So after the Flood, the gods decided to delegate the power over every-day human life to their decedents born by the daughters of men, making them city-kings. Meanwhile, the Nephilim themselves relocated to the city temples, becoming deities for the mortals called "Black-Headed."

Chapter 3 of *Genesis* reports a conversation in Eden between the serpent and the woman, in front of Adam. The serpent, who "*was more subtle than any beast of the field,*" tells the woman: "**Yea, hath God said, Ye shall not eat of every tree of the garden?**"

The woman interrupts him, saying, "**We may eat of the fruit of the trees of the garden. But of the fruit of the tree which is in the midst of the garden, God hath said, Ye shall not eat of it, neither shall ye touch it, lest ye die.**" (*Genesis* 3:2-3).

Eventually, the serpent manages to convince the woman: "***Ye shall not surely die. For God doth know that in the day ye eat thereof, then your eyes shall be opened, and ye shall be as gods, knowing good and evil.***"

She cannot resist the temptation, yet, being a woman, takes her time, since she needs more arguments to overcome her fear of God. First, she explores and experiments: "***And when the woman saw that the tree was good for food, and that it was pleasant to the eyes, and a tree to be desired to make one wise, she took of the fruit thereof, and did eat, and gave also unto her husband with her***"; (*Genesis* 3:6). Then, suddenly, "***And the eyes of them both were opened, and they knew that they were naked***" (*Genesis* 3:7). End of the age of innocence indeed: Man was forced out of Eden, barred from return, "**[L]est he put forth his hand, and take also of the tree of life, and eat, and live forever**" (*Genesis* 3:22).

These are the very words of Enlil, in the equivalent Sumerian text. Enlil keeps looking for ways to get rid of man, until the Flood is about to begin. The Assembly of gods meets, approving Enlil's statement, similar to "***I will sweep the man whom***

I have created from the face of the Earth": (*Genesis* 6:7). As opposed to him, Enki hoped his creation would grow and become intelligent, and eat the fruit of tree of knowledge. So, despite the decision of the Assembly, Enki, (another participant in the Creation of Man), also known as the serpent, breaks the news about the next Flood to one man, advising him to build an ark (see Illustration 7).

Z. Sitchin

Illustration 7: Enki, also known as "the serpent," warns Noah, about the Flood's coming.

Though one can always find new or additional meanings in texts, no conclusion can contradict all previous conclusions. Yet in this case the allusions are numerous and disguised rather thinly. Rabbi Akiva was the only one to have ventured into the Garden and leave unharmed, because he grasped the Zeitgeist of the reported events, and was familiar with the convictions of the God-fearing people, that if God wills, He could afflict a curse on the serpent. Akiva was also aware of the constraints of the writers who tried to deliver the simple monotheistic message that only one god exists while the Bible mentions that God "***standeth in the congregation of the mighty, judges among the gods***" (*Psalms* 82:1). Mentioned here as part of its many narratives, the twelve members of Sumerian Pantheon, including **Bel/Marduk/Lord**, the chief deity during the early Babylonian and Assyrian kingdoms. At the same time, he was also the dominant god, exerting his influence on Earth and interfering with all its historical events.

CHAPTER 4:

THE NEPHILIM WERE ON EARTH

As we mentioned, the Nephilim ruled the Earth through a Pantheon of twelve selected gods, who decided to lord over mankind. This is what is meant by "***God standeth in the congregation of the mighty, judges among the gods***" (*Psalms* 82:1). The chief deities of the congregation were three who came from heaven, from the planet Nibiru, with 600 of the Nephilim. That family was headed by Anu, the chief deity of the Nephilim and the ruler of Nibiru. He landed on Earth accompanied by his two sons, Enlil and Enki, two ancestors who had sons and daughters born on Earth, and assumed positions in the Pantheon by order of appearance. As the tablets in the creation story chapter shows, each of the twelve Gods of Heaven, that is the twelve solar system bodies, were associated with one of the twelve Gods of Heaven and Earth, that is, the Nephilim Pantheon members.

Sumerian historical texts frequently mention the deities' names, especially those dating from the Neo-Sumerian Empire, when the aforementioned twelve gods established themselves as Pantheon members. The Bible also refers to them, when reporting times when the gods participated in, and affected, events, interfering with human lives. Each deity is referred to through its prominent features, its role in the congregation, and its effect on the historic period of one's activity. This allows a description and categorization of the deities and their qualities.

The biblical God is presented as a vengeful God, visiting the sins of fathers on their sons, etc., kind to His followers and to those observant of His commandments. While other deities are mere pieces of wood and stone, the Hebrew God is portrayed as the only one familiar with the secrets of a human heart: "***If we have forgotten the name of our God, or stretched out our hands to a strange god; Shall not God search this out? For he knoweth the secrets of the heart***" (*Psalms* 44:21). The Sumerian texts and images present each of the deities together with one's peculiar features, and field of activity. The following is a list of them and their features, as reported in the numerous early Sumerian texts and images dealing with the gods:

1. **Apsu**: As mentioned above, its name comes from "abyss," here referring to deep space. Its god was **Shamash**. Its original Sumerian name has nothing to do with *shemesh*, the Hebrew word for sun. Writers accepted the god's Akkadian name, Utu—"shining," as the name for the heavenly body called the Sun, associated with *shamash*. On Earth, Shamash was a young prominent Neo-Sumerian deity, in charge of space travel, control towers and telecommunication facilities in the airports of Dilmun, in Sinai. His main and permanent residence was in the City of the Sun, or Heliopolis, currently Baalbek, Lebanon, in a temple the magnificent ruins of which had survived to amaze us. Shamash was the son of Nanar/Sin, the Moon god; he was the twin brother of Inanna/Ishtar, the biblical Ashtoreth. All three enjoyed the strongest influence during the Third Kingdom of Ur, until its collapse at about 2024 B.C.E.

    The following are translated fragments from the *Hymn to Shamash*:[1]
    Shamash illuminates the darkness, judge of heaven;
    Which are the mountains not clothed with your beams?
    Regularly and without cease you traverse the heavens,
    Every day you pass over the broad Earth....
    Shamash, there confronts you the caravan, those journeying in fear,
    The traveling merchant, the agent who is carrying capital.
    Shamash, there confronts you the fisherman with his net,
    The roving dead, the vagrant soul,
    They confront you, Shamash, and you hear all.
    You destroy the horns of a scheming villain,
    You observe, Shamash, prayer, supplication, and benediction,
    Obeisance, kneeling, ritual murmurs, and prostration.
    They in their reverence laud the mention of you,
    And worship your majesty forever.

---

[1] Translation by W. G. Lambert from his book *Babylonian Wisdom Literature*, (Oxford, 1960). I, 127 ff.

2. **Mummu**: (Mercury) The smallest solar system heavenly body, its size 0.056 times that of Earth. It was the first to have been repulsed by the explosion of Apsu/Sun, and remained the closest to it in the system. Its god was Ishkur the Sumerian, the equivalent of Haddad the Akkadian, son of Enlil. Known as the storm god, Ishkur was attributed with many powers. Being the uncle of the twin siblings Utu and Inanna, and the brother of the Moon god, Sin, he was a member of a foursome who enjoyed much renown all over the ancient Near East, mostly because of the endless bitter rivalry and conflicts between the family of his father, Enlil, and the family of Enki. In the Hittite Kingdom he was known as god **Teshub**, "the wind-blower."

3. **Tiamat/Enlil:** Together with his father, Anu and his brother Enki, landed on Earth accompanied by a great number of Nephilim about half a million years ago. Among them, Enlil was the most powerful and prominent, being the eldest son of Anu, chief of the Sumerian Pantheon. When the domains of the Earth were divided between the brothers, Enlil was allotted a region called **E. Din.**, that is, "House of Justice," (the biblical Eden, between the Euphrates and Tigris rivers), where most important matters of the Earth were managed. The lot of Enki, his brother, was the netherworld, that is, the Western Hemisphere with all its oceans. There, he was named E. A. - e=house, a= water; or "water dweller." It was mostly this distancing of Enki from the scene of major affairs on Earth that triggered the sibling rivalry, which, over the years, was passed on to their decedents, in both dynasties. Enlil was one of the first gods to have landed on Earth from their abode on planet Nibiru, and should be accredited as the initiator and realizer of civilization, culture and social order on Earth. His permanent residence was in the city of Nippur, one of the first seven cities founded by the Nephilim on the shore of the Persian Gulf. It was considered a sacred city, the site of *Dur An Ki*, or "link between heaven and earth." The decision to start the Flood, reported in *Genesis* 6:7: "***And it repented the LORD that he had made man on the Earth, and it grieved him at his heart. I will destroy man whom I have created from the face of the Earth***," is associated with Enlil. But according to Sumerian texts, the Nephilim knew about the Flood in advance and therefore held an Assembly of the gods who decided to keep the news secret from man, so he would perish in the Flood. Enki, being the brother of Enlil, who personally participated in the Creation of Man, having pity

on this creature, betrayed the secret to Utnapishtim, (the equivalent of Noah of the Flood), advising him to build an ark, or ship, to save himself and his family from the Flood. Sumerian texts have it that the gods' hostility towards mankind had started long before, particularly on the part of Enlil, the chief deity of the Nephilim, residing in E. Din, (the biblical Eden, in Mesopotamia); He could not stand the troubles caused by the Black-Headed, as mortals were then referred to. They depended on the gods for everything, and made noise disturbing the peace of Enlil. He also predicted what was to become of that creature: "[L]est *he put forth his hand, and take also of the tree of life, and eat, and live forever*" (*Genesis* 3:22). Enki, Enlil's brother, who was allotted with dominion over the netherworld, that is, the Western Hemisphere, served as the chief science officer of the Nephilim, producing minerals out of the oceans, gold mining in Africa and starting the hospitals of the Nephilim. His icon was the snake, the symbol of medicine ever since, and he was also known as the serpent. Involved in the Creation of Man, he cared for his mind's child, wishing him to acquire knowledge and develop his skills. Therefore, the serpent said to the woman, after she had eaten the fruit of the Tree of Knowledge: "**Ye shall not surely die: For God doth know that in the day ye eat thereof, then your eyes shall be opened, and ye shall be as gods, knowing good and evil.**" (*Genesis* 3: 4-5). Thus, Enlil is associated with the Tree of Life, while Enki, the serpent, with the Tree of Knowledge (see also Illustration 7). After the Flood, Enlil accepted mankind's survival of the destruction and started to establish a social order regulated by progressive laws protecting the rights of humans. Tiamat, his planet, was initially covered with water. According to the Enuma Elish creation epic, as a result of a collision between planet Nibiru and Tiamat, the latter came to be planet Earth, mother of all living creatures. Hence the Sumerian word "gi," or "ki," which means *terra firma* (similar to the Greek, Gaia).

A lament addressed to Enlil strongly reflects a cataclysm suffered by Sumer in 2024 B.C.E., after which Marduk was made its chief deity:

The lord of all the lands has abandoned it, the land is bewildered;
Enlil, the prince, abandoned it, the land is bewildered;
In a city damned by its lord, The queen cries bitterly,
uttering a woe, wailing A city forsaken by its lord,
A city Enlil abandoned to the storm.

The house of Nippur is utterly destroyed;
The shrine of Ekur is utterly destroyed;
The shrine of Babylonia is utterly destroyed,
Brickwork of Ur is utterly destroyed;
The Esagila was utterly destroyed;
The Temple Ezida was utterly destroyed;
The shrine of Borsippa was utterly destroyed;

Reduced his land to ruin;
He swept the winds over the black-headed people
The reaping storm dragged across the land' and
Like a flood storm it completely destroyed the city.

The field grows tangled weed.

1. **Lahmu:** Associated with **Nabu**, son of Marduk and the grandson of Enki, of the last sons of gods of the third generation to have joined the Pantheon of the Twelve. He gave his name to Mount Nebo, east of Jericho. He was a daring warrior, the equivalent of Mars. Appropriately, Lahmu was Mars, the first outer planet after Earth. It is larger than Mercury, 0.150 times the size of Earth.

2. **Lahamu:** Venus—associated with the warrior goddess Inanna. Her symbol was depicted as an eight-horned star. It is slightly smaller than Earth, 0.857 times the size of the latter. She was the Canaanite-Egyptian Ishtar/Ashtoreth, the twin sister of Utu/Shamash, the major goddess during the Third Kingdom of Ur. Together with her brother, Utu, and her father Sin, the Moon god, they ruled a central domain, stretching from Egypt in the west to Indus Valley in the east. The texts dealing with events of that period cover the very early fifteen hundred years of her rule in the city of Uruk, the biblical Erech. Inanna was considered the goddess of love and war alike, occupying a prominent position among the Gods of Heaven and Earth. Using her beauty and charms, she made her way to prominence in the Pantheon, assuming a domain that included Egypt. There, the chief deity was Amon/Ra, the same as Marduk. **Amon-Ra** son of Enki, forced by Inanna to flee all the way to Antalya plains, where he founded the Hittite Kingdom; The Indus Valley, too, was within the domain of Inanna, and she used to pay occasional visits there using her spacecraft. Ancient texts always list the seven objects she used to wear on her travels, all of which have something to do with aviation:

1. The **SHUGARRA** she put on her head.
2. "**Measuring pendants**," on her ears.
3. **Chains of small blue stones**, around her neck.
4. Twin "**stones**" on her shoulders.
5. A golden **cylinder**, in her hands.
6. **Straps**, clasping her breast.
7. The **PALA garment**, clothed around her body.

"**The SHUGARRA**" (similar to "shigur," or "shidur," Hebrew for "transmission") was a helmet fitted with horns, probably antennas used for transmitting communication.

"**Measuring pendants**," were probably to stabilize her head during take-off.

The chain of stones, or a breastplate, is similar to the one worn by the High Priest in the Tabernacle. It contained 12 stones, serving for communication at different frequencies.

The "**Twin stones**," served to minimize the spacecraft's gravity during climbing.

The "**golden cylinder**," judging by its thickness, seems like some device directing the craft in space.

The "**Straps**" served to fasten some object to her back, probably a parachute.

"**The PALA garment**" was certainly a standard pilot's suit.

6. **Anshar:** ("Lord of Heaven") was associated with Ninurta, eldest son of Enlil born of his mistress Ninhursag. Therefore, he claimed himself the eldest son and intended successor of Enlil as the chief of the Pantheon of the Twelve. Yet Marduk, another son of Enki, proclaimed himself as the favorite son, arguing he was the eldest since primogeniture goes to the genuine wife's son. This started bitter hostility and struggles between the two families, lasting until the second millennium B.C.E. Anshar, or Saturn, is one of the largest solar system planets, a fact always mentioned by the ancients who were well acquainted with the solar system. Its volume is 800 times that of planet Earth.

7. **Kishar:** ("Lord of the Earth"), associated with Nergal, son of Enki, whose main activity was in the netherworld of Western Hemisphere, in the gold and uranium mines ruled by his wife, Ereshkigal, sister of Inanna/Ishtar. Kishar is Jupiter, the largest solar system planet, with a volume 1200 times that of Earth.

8. **Anu**: (From "An," or heaven") Chief of the Sumerian Pantheon and ruler of Nibiru, from where he came to Earth with his two sons, Enlil and Enki, and six hundred Anunnaki. "An" means "heaven" and "ki" means "Earth." Therefore, they are "those who came down from heaven to Earth, the very same as the Nephilim ("those who fell") referred to in *Joshua* ; "father of Anak" mentioned in Numbers 21:11. The planet associated with Anu is Uranus.

9. **Nudimmud**: Nickname of Enki, the chief science officer of the Nephilim, in charge of medicine and called "the serpent," symbol of medicine. He participated in the Creation of Man, out of an egg cell of a hominid fertilized with the sperm of Nephilim and implanted in the womb of one of their daughters. The newborn was a new type of creature, called *Lulu Amelu* (see "Enki and Ninmach," the Creation of Man" in - *In Those Distant Days, Anthology of Mesopotamian Literature in Hebrew*, by Shin Shifra and Jacob Klein, p.83). Ea, also known as Enki, was one of the major gods to have landed on Earth, with his father Anu and brother. His name means "water-dweller," because when the gods divided the dominion of Earth, he was allotted the netherworld, the Western Hemisphere, where the oceans were. He also ruled Africa with its gold and uranium mines. According to ancient texts, the Assembly of Nephilim forbade any intimate association with the daughters of men. Enki/Ea was the first to have broken this prohibition, being closely associated with the wife of Lamech, father of Noah of the Flood. Enki was the god who revealed to Noah that the Flood was nigh, advising him to build a vessel in order to save his family.

10. **Kingu**: Sumerian Kingu is Akkadian Nanar/Sin, the largest of the eleven satellites of Tiamat. Scientists had long ago concluded that Kingu, the Moon, was a planet in the making, confirming the meaning of what Enuma Elish epic says:"**She placed the Tablets of Destinies on his breast**," the "Tablets of Destinies" being its position and orbit around the Sun. According to the Enuma Elish creation story, Tiamat promoted Kingu to lead the Celestial Battle and mustered the host of her guardian satellites to fight the gods who had decided to destroy them.

11. **Gaga** was associated with Pluto, the planet smaller than Saturn situated near it, which was considered to be his minister. It is associated with god Dumuzi/Tammuz, son of Enki and husband and lover of Inanna, united with her in a marriage reconciling the two rival families.

12. **Marduk** was associated with Nibiru, a planet which, according to Mesopotamian Creation epic, was formed in deep space and trapped by the combined gravity of the solar system (see Z. Sitchin's *The Twelfth Planet,* p.172, figure 99). In 2024 B.C.E., a major cataclysm hit Sumer, forcing the gods to leave their abodes on Earth; Marduk was the only god unaffected by it, since he was attending his affairs far in the north, in the Hittite Kingdom, on the shores of Black Sea. After the gods had returned to Earth, Marduk was made the chief of Sumerian Pantheon, and the chronicles were modified. Following Marduk's demand, planet Nibiru was renamed Marduk, after the chief of Sumerian Pantheon.

The Nephilim established the first civilization on Earth. They founded cities and led ordinary lives with their people performing all kinds of work, including the hardest menial tasks of mining gold and other minerals in Africa. Eventually, it proved unbearably difficult even to the children of Nephilim, who decided to revolt. Well acquainted with the possibilities offered by the advanced technology of genetic engineering, they demanded a solution from their leaders. It was submitted to god Enki, who was, as we said, the chief science officer of the Nephilim. After some consideration, he concluded that the solution already existed. All it took was the creation of the hominid or Neanderthal, with the spirit of the gods. What was needed was to make a "Lulu Amelu," or a laboring savage, to relieve the Nephilim of all hard labor. Enki, who was also in charge of the healing of Nephilim, undertook to create a solution, that is, a creature capable of carrying out all the difficult mining tasks. Thus, the Nephilim decided to create man through genetic engineering manipulation, namely fertilizing female hominid egg cells with their semen and implanting into female Nephilim.

The two dynasties of Nephilim had ruled the Earth until 2024 B.C.E. They warred with each other, competing for influence and trying to win over tribes, nations and other groups of humans whom they had called "black-headed."

By the middle of the third millennium B.C.E., the Third Empire of Ur was at its zenith, its center in Ur ruled by the family of god Sin and his two twin sons, namely Utu/Shamash and Inanna/Ishtar (see Illustration 8). The Kingdom was expanded eastward, as far as the Indus Valley. In the west, Ishtar forced Marduk out of Egypt, making him flee to Antalya plains, where he founded the Hittite Kingdom. In 2024 B.C.E., the Third Kingdom of Ur came to an end, following a bitter struggle between the two dynasties, giving rise to the kingdoms of Akkad, Assyria and Babylonia, headed by god Marduk. He was made chief deity, and ruled the Earth until the Nephilim left around 200 B.C.E. All documented historical events since were conducted his way, as can be inferred from the following biblical verses:

The LORD rideth upon a swift cloud, and came unto Egypt: and the idols of Egypt shall be moved at his presence, and the heart of Egypt shall melt in the midst of it: (Isaiah 19:1)

In that day shall there be a highway out of Egypt to Assyria, and the Assyrian shall come unto Egypt, and the Egyptian unto Assyria, and the Egyptians shall be enslaved to the Assyrians. (Isaiah 19:23)

Behold, I will send and take all the families of the north, saith the LORD, and Nebuchadnezzar king of Babylon my servant, (Jeremiah 25:9)

And now have I given all these lands into the hand of Nebuchadnezzar the king of Babylon, my servant; (Jeremiah 27:6)

And I will set Egyptians against Egyptians: and they shall fight every one against his brother, and every one against his neighbour; city against city, and kingdom against kingdom. (Isaiah 19:2)

Thus saith the LORD to his anointed, to Cyrus (Isaiah 45:1)

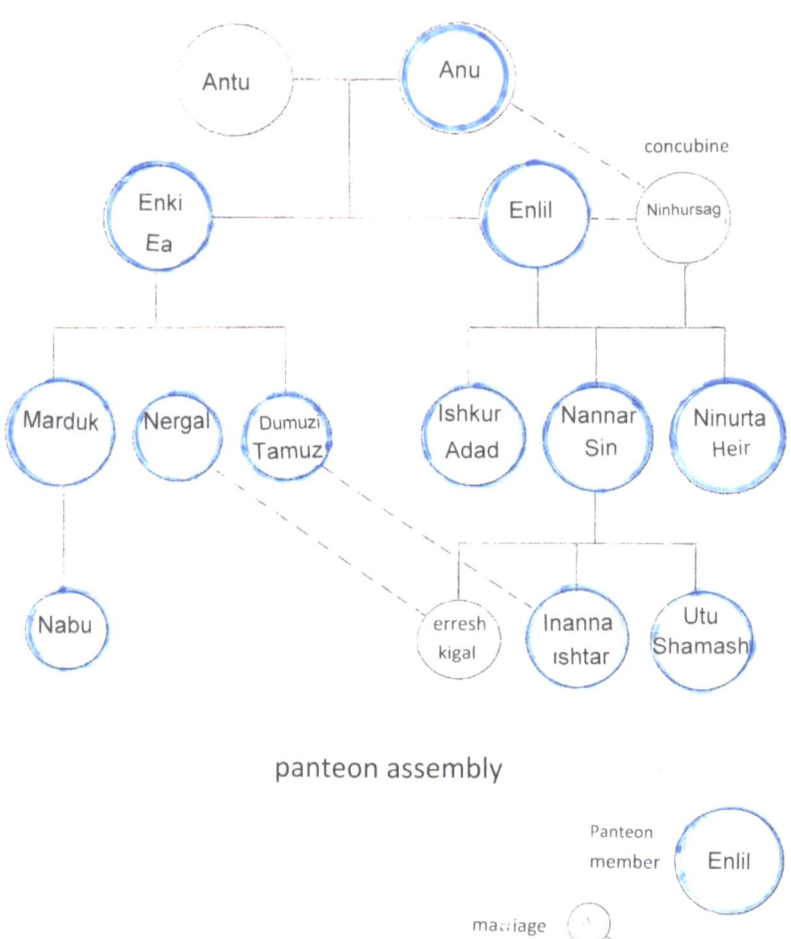

Illustration 8

CHAPTER 5

THE FLOOD | WATER UPON EARTH

According to the Bible, Yahweh decided to punish mankind: "***And it repented the LORD that he had made man on the Earth, and it grieved him at his heart.***" (*Genesis* 6:6). Then, he decides to wipe out every creature on Earth with the Flood to come: ***And, behold, I, even I, do bring a flood of waters upon the Earth, to destroy all flesh*** (ibid., 6:17). As far as both humans and every living thing on Earth are concerned, there is one god. According to ancient texts, the Nephilim had managed to foresee the Flood, a disastrous cataclysm submerging Earth with water and making all living things on Earth perish. Though the biblical narrative offers little detail on this major event, scientists have concluded it was no mere seasonal flood during local rainy season, but rather a unique event, wreaking destruction on everything that lived on Earth. The water flowed from southwest, covering the five-thousand meter high Ararat Mountain, where Noah's Ark eventually rested after the water level had started dropping and land was seen.

The numerous Sumerian texts discovered by archaeologists also tell us about the antediluvian as well as postdiluvian periods. Thus, the Pentateuch interpretations are nothing more than the literal meaning of the pre-biblical texts, which were unconstrained by any religious doctrine. They tell us about the gods interfering with the events, as well as their association with mortals. They show references to mysteries with much puzzlement and questions about all the stages of the event, as well as on what befell the characters involved during the period following the Flood.

"But Noah found grace in the eyes of the LORD" (ibid., 6:8).

Who was Noah? Why did he find grace in the eyes of the Lord? The Bible offers no further information on him, except that he was born to Lamech, son of Methuselah, and found grace in the eyes of Yahweh. According to biblical genealogy, Noah was the tenth generation descendant of Adam. Mesopotamian chronicles indicate there were ten rulers who had landed on Earth before the

Flood, whose total reign amounted to four hundred and thirty-two thousand years, which are 120 Shars, or Nibiruan years. Nine of the rulers were of the Nephilim, while the tenth was Ubartutu, also known as Lamech, father of Noah. The latter was son of a mortal woman who was impregnated by one of the Nephilim, sons of gods, according to *Genesis* 6: "**That the sons of God saw the daughters of men that they were fair; and they took them wives of all which they chose.**" Right afterward, the Bible says that Yahweh repented the creation of man, aiming to wipe him out from Earth, as well as all fowl and beasts. According to ancient texts, the Nephilim had learned about the future Flood, and prepared to leave Earth in their spacecraft together, at a preset time.

When Noah asked how would he know when to embark his ship, Enki tells him to look north at sunset, towards the city of Nippur, where he would see a burst of lights in the sky. That meant the Nephilim gathered in their spacecraft, and were ordered to take off at the predetermined time. That takeoff sheds light from far away. Ancient narratives report, in detail, how Inanna/Ishtar stood next to the stern of a spacecraft, looking on with tearful eyes at the creatures below who were carried away by the torrents of the Flood. It was god Enki who told Noah about the coming Flood (see Illustration 7), suggesting Noah to leave everything and build a vessel to save himself and his kin. So, one may wonder how Noah was associated with the god. When the gods found out about the increasingly numerous relations between the Nephilim and daughters of men, as reported by *Genesis* 6, their Assembly met, forbidding any contacts with these women. According to ancient texts, Enki had been closely associated with the family of Methuselah, and therefore, Enki was punished as well.

According to a deciphered passage of the Qumran Scrolls, when Lamech first saw his son Noah, he was amazed to find him blue-eyed and white-faced. Unlike all mortals, who had been black-faced and therefore referred to as "black-headed," newborn Noah had fair skin and eyes. The segment reads:

"***Behold, I thought in my heart that the conception was of the Watchers, and the pregnancy of the Holy Ones and the Nephilim. Therefore, I hastily came to my wife, Bat Enosh, saying: I attest about you by the Supreme One, the Lord and King of All Worlds.***"

Thus, the documented history confirms the unbroken link between the Bible and earlier texts of Sumer, biblical Shinar. This text also suggests an answer to why Noah found grace in the eyes of Yahweh. Hence, one can also draw conclusions about the ten generations from Shem, son of Noah, to Abram, later Abraham. "Ab-ram," literally meaning "prominent father," refers to his father Terah, a prominent man; he served as a high priest of the temple built by Ishtar/Ashtoreth in honor of her father, Moon-god Sin, or Sumerian Kingu, in the Third Kingdom of Ur (4th millennium to late 2nd millennium B.C.E.). Abraham and his geostrategic role in the region are referred to in the next chapter, "Abraham in the Service of the Gods."

Back to the Flood: as we said, the Nephilim had known it was to take place.

Z. Sitchin in *The Twelfth Planet* argues it was the end of an ice age turning nearly one-third of the Earth into Antarctica. The enormous mass of glaciers, up to thousands of meters high, generated intense heat at its bottom layer, turning it slippery. Planet Nibiru approaching Earth, on its distant elliptical orbit, and the former's gravitational force, made the glaciers collapse at once, thus raising the surface of oceans, immersing the land around them. The only recently deciphered ancient texts dealing with the Flood demonstrate an astonishing similarity to chapters of the biblical narrative, as well as answers to many questions, mysteries and dilemmas raised by later biblical ethos in an attempt to modify these texts to Israelite legacy and Jewish religious doctrine.

The Flood is reported, in full detail, in the *Epic of Gilgamesh*, King of Uruk, from middle of the third millennium B.C.E., as Gilgamesh had heard it from the Sumerian version of Noah. Gilgamesh, closely related to the god Shamash, the one in charge of spaceflights, addressed the latter during his quest for eternity:

*The ruler Gilgamesh
Toward the Land of Dilmun set his mind.*

*Let me enter the Land,
Let me set up my shem.
In the places where the shems are raised up,
Let me raise my shem....
Bring me to the landing place...*

Z. Sitchin

Illustration 9: The line across separates from above ground with the triangle, and a pit underground, and a rocket of tree compartments.

Dilmun was a secured area serving as a spaceflight center, complete with runways, control tower and other facilities situated in Sinai, an area ruled by god Shamash. When planet Nibiru came close to the Sun, on his distant elliptical orbit, Dilmun served as the departure point of regular roundtrip flights between the planet of the Nephilim and Earth. The tomb of a senior Egyptian official in charge of Sinai, contained items he used on duty. A mural found in the tomb is shown in Figure 9. The line drawn across the painting separates the aboveground part and a pit occupying most of the lower part. There, one can see the larger part of a two-stage rocket containing tree compartments of different functions. In its lower part, one can see two astronauts at work. The part seen above ground bears an astonishing resemblance to the command module in which Neil Armstrong landed in the ocean on his flight back from the Moon. So, one may assume that the first landing of the Nephilim on Earth took place at sea. On the sides of the pit, the rocket's exhaust gases are depicted as two leopard skins.

Genesis 14 reports on a great war between the four kings of Shinar, on one hand, and five kings of Canaan assembled at Kadesh Bar-ne'a, Sinai, on the other hand. The chapter dealing with Abraham refers to ancient texts presenting the role Abraham played in that war, as well as evidence that Dilmun, or Tilmun, was Sinai, rather than modern Bahrain, as scholars misidentify it.

Fortunately for Gilgamesh, the god provided him with a *shem*, or spacecraft, and an astronaut to fly it. The numerous texts dealing with it offer an amazingly vivid description of the takeoff, the increasingly shrinking sight of Earth the higher the spacecraft climbs, and the many perils facing a space traveler: the two men cross the asteroid belt, and the ship being shaken by cosmic storms. Finally, after an arduous and adventurous journey, the craft reached its destination, namely planet Nibiru, where Gilgamesh meets Noah. One may assume such a statement provokes challenging questions, heresy, dilemmas and denial of several religious beliefs and age-old traditions, as well as conclusions incompatible with current knowledge. Yet the answers to all these questions are even more amazing. The meeting of these two fails to provide answers to all questions. Though, one can find from the numerous texts dealing with the event, answers to many fundamental questions such as whether or not Noah was taken to the Planet of the Nephilim on board a craft; how long he stayed there and what happened to him; what happened to Gilgamesh, and how the latter was received by Noah. Gilgamesh recounts the events as told to him by Noah, about god Enlil descending to Earth when he saw Noah's Ark resting on Mount Ararat:

Thereupon Enlil went aboard the ship.

Holding me by the hand, he took me aboard.

He took my wife aboard and made (her) kneel by my side.

Standing between us, he touched our foreheads to bless us:

'Hitherto Utnapishtim has been but human.

Henceforth Utnapishtim and his wife shall be like unto us gods.

Utnapishtim shall reside far away, at the mouth of the rivers!'

Thus they took me and made me reside far away,

At the mouth of the rivers.

'As for you, Gilgamesh, who will assemble the gods for your sake, so that you may find that life for which you are searching? Wake up, after sleeping for seven days and seven nights. But while Gilgamesh sat there resting on his haunches, a mist of sleep drifted over him like storm.'

This is what Noah tells Gilgamesh, adding that Gilgamesh fell asleep for six days and seven nights. Not solely the journey exhausted Gilgamesh; he arrived at a world where time is measured differently. As we have already explained, time is affected by the distance from the Sun. So, by our calculations, six Nibiruan days are equivalent to sixty-nine Earth years. Therefore, it takes time for human physiology to adapt to a new temporal environment. According to ancient texts, Gilgamesh failed to adapt, and took a journey back to Earth. Following him right away, Noah and his family, too, returned to Earth, resettling it (see map below).

The expansion of Noah sons after the flood

How long did Noah, his wife and three sons stay on planet Nibiru? There is no reference to that found in Sumerian texts. But *Genesis* 12, the chapter dealing with the dissemination of humanity in the post-Flood Near East, offers an intriguing hint:

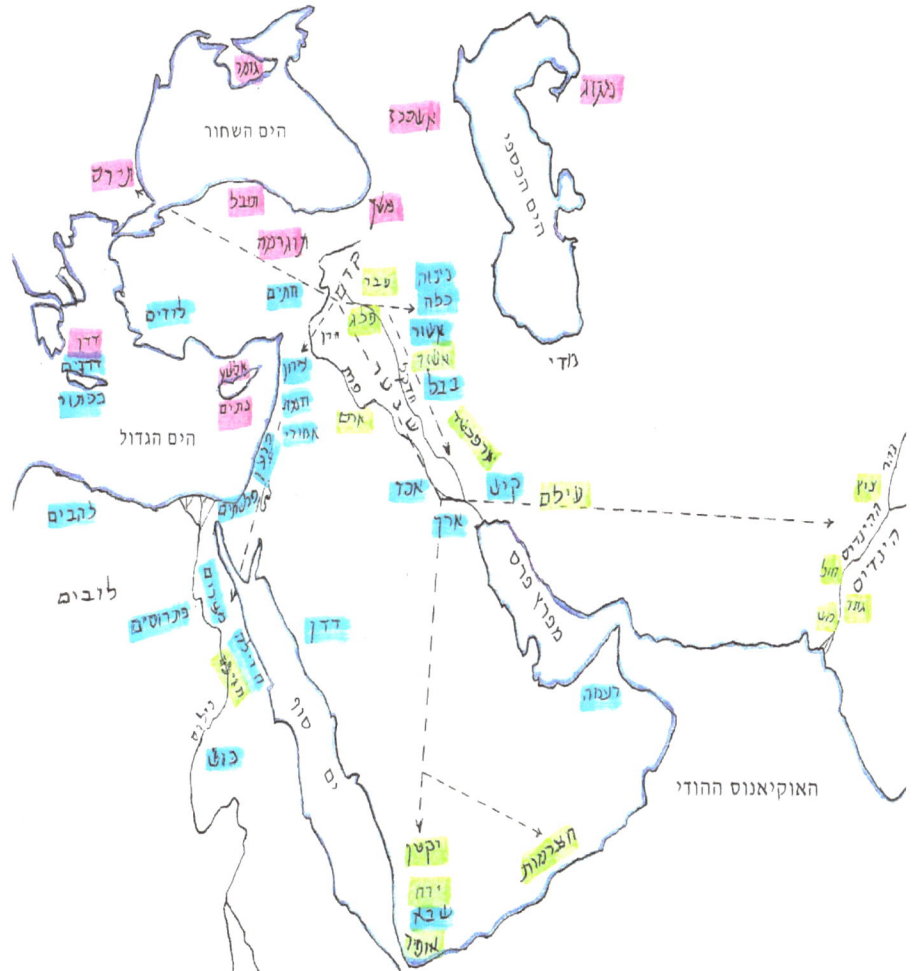

"*These are the generations of Shem: Shem was an hundred years old, and begat Arphaxad two years after the flood*" (*Genesis* 11:10). Later in the text, there are ten generations of descendants of Shem mentioned, down to Abraham, with each person's age at which he bore his son. Their sum total amounts to three hundred and ninety-two years. By comparison, Abraham was seventy-five years old when Yahweh told him:

"***Get thee out of thy country, and from thy kindred, and from thy father's house, unto a land that I will show thee***" (*Genesis* 12:1).

Judging from contemporary texts, it had something to do with the war of the four kings of Shinar against the five kings of Canaan, back in 2048 B.C.E. Therefore, basic arithmetic shows that Abraham was born in 2123 B.C.E. (2048 plus 75). Adding the 392 years back to Shem, son of Noah, we get 2515 years, that is, mid-third millennium B.C.E. Thus, there are 7500 years missing from the beginning of the 11th millennium B.C.E. How can such a miscalculation of time have been made in the Bible? Calculating more accurately, we add to Abraham's birth year just 390 years, since two years after the flood were the Nibiru years. Now, the result is 2513 B.C.E. Adding two years on Nibiru, that is, 7200 Earth years, we get 9713 B.C.E. Now we find there are 1283 years missing until the 11th millennium B.C.E., when the Flood took place, that is, one-third of a Nibiruan year. To conclude: Shem bore Arphaxad when he returned to Earth 8525 years after the Flood, about two and a half years in Nephilim time, an insignificant difference. Indeed, one may get the impression that the Bible confirms Pre-biblical lore.

"***And the LORD said unto Noah, … Of every clean beast thou shalt take to thee by sevens, the male and his female; and of beasts that are not clean by two, the male and his female.***" (*Genesis* 7:1-2)

So, seven males and females of each clean beast were taken onboard for the reproduction and feeding of Noah and his family for the year and ten days they spent aboard the Ark, according to the Bible. The Bible offers no explanation on how the unclean beasts survived, though some well-known modern artists depict a ramp rising to the Ark, on which all animals walk in pairs - a bull and his cow elephant, a fox and his vixen, a lion with a lioness, and even the serpent and his mate. But today, technological progress and genetic engineering discoveries allow one to assume that the Nephilim, with intelligence far surpassing that of humans, then and now, could have worked out a cleverer solution. And indeed, according to the texts reporting the instructions to mankind about the preparations for the future Flood, god Enki/Ea, who had betrayed to Noah the secret of the Flood, addressed the "***son of Ubar-Tutu***," (the equivalent of biblical Lamech, father of Noah), ordering him to take onboard "***the seed of all livings***":

Man of Shuruppak, son of Ubar-Tutu,
Tear down (this) house, build a ship!

Give up possessions, seek thou life.

Despise property and keep the soul alive.

Aboard the ship take thou **the seed of all living.**

The ship that thou shalt build,
Her dimensions shall be to measure.

After the building of the ship had been accomplished with the help of the people of Shuruppak, Noah entered the ship with his wife, sons and their wives; then, "***in the second month, the seventeenth day of the month, the same day were all the fountains of the great deep broken up, and the windows of heaven were opened.***" (*Genesis* 7:11), the water flowed both beneath and above the Ark, raining from above and sweeping the water... according to Sumerian texts, forced the waters of Tigris and Euphrates northward, carrying the Ark towards Mount Ararat.

"**And in the second month, on the seven and twentieth day of the month, was the Earth dried**" (*Genesis* 8:14). It happened on the sixth hundred and first year of Noah's life, which means the ordeal lasted for one year and ten days. Then Noah and everybody who was with him came out of the Ark. Noah erected an altar and made burned offerings: "**And the LORD smelled a sweet savour; and the LORD said in his heart, I will not again curse the ground any more for man's sake; for the imagination of man's heart is evil from his youth;**" (*Genesis* 8:11). The happy ending is diametrically opposed to the entire narrative of the Flood, which starts with a long condemnation of human kind for various transgressions, including the violation of innocence by young gods. Against this background, the decision to end all flesh seems absolutely reasonable and justifiable. Yet then, the very same god is charmed by the sweet scent rising from the altar, forgetting his earlier resolution to exterminate humanity and concludes the story by forgiving humanity, while condemning man for the evil imagination of his heart from his youth, rather than condemning the young gods for taking wives from among the daughters of men. But the doubts about the inner logic of the narrative are resolved once we realize the message of the biblical narrative is an edited version of the Sumerian original. As in similar cases, here, too, the monotheistic Bible combined in one god the poles played by many deities, who had not always acted in accordance with each other. Until Mesopotamian civilization had been discovered and Sumerian and Akkadian literature understood, the biblical version of the Flood had only been supported by some sporadic primitive myths. The discovery of the *Epic of Gilgamesh* promoted the biblical Flood narrative into the prestigious company of ancient texts, even more exulted once fragments of the Sumerian original had been discovered. The protagonist of the Mesopotamian Flood was named *Ziusudra* in Sumerian and *Utnapishtim* in Akkadian. After the Flood, he was taken to reside in the abode of gods. When Gilgamesh, on his quest for eternity, arrived there and met Utnapishtim, he asked him for advice on matters of life and death. It was then that Utnapishtim revealed to Gilgamesh, and, through him all post-diluvian mankind, the secret of his survival; "***a secret thing, a mystery of the gods***"- the true story of the Flood. That secret was that before the Flood the gods, headed by Enlil, held a meeting and voted for destroying mankind. Though the vote and resolution were kept secret, Enki was looking for Utnapishtim, or Noah, to warn him about the future disaster. Eventually, he spoke to Utnapishtim confidentially, through a screen of reeds. First, the secret revealed seemed enigmatic, but later he offered clearer caution and advice. The similarities to the biblical narrative are evident: a Flood is about to take place; one man is warned to save himself by building a ship and taking his kin onboard to save humanity. Yet the Mesopotamian version makes more sense: here, the decisions to perish and the attempt to save are not contradictory actions of the same deity. Rather, one god, Enki, secretly defying the unanimous resolution made by the Assembly of great gods, carries out the warning and attempt to save the seed of man.

Once again, one realizes that the ancient texts mention several gods involved in the narrative of the Flood. Earlier chapters discussed the twelve members of Pantheon who dominated Earth, whose names are mentioned scattered all over the Bible, let alone the biblical references to groups of gods, in the plural form, such as the following:

"***And God said, Let us make man in our image, after our likeness***" (*Genesis*1:26);

"***God standeth in the congregation of the mighty; he judgeth among the gods***"(*Psalms* 82:1);

"***Among the gods there is none like unto thee, O Lord***" (*Psalms* 86:8).

Here it is to be noted that, as we have demonstrated in the chapter dealing with the creation story, it is actually two deities. The Enuma Elish creation myth mentions by name all twelve members of the Sumerian Pantheon, the same as the congregation of the mighty referred to in *Psalms*. It was headed by god Bel/Marduk/Lord, the same as Yahweh. It is also confirmed by the words of Prophet Jeremiah about "**King of Babylonia, my servant**," whose Lord was god Bel; King of Assyria whose Lord was Ashur ("the seer"); and Egypt; where the chief deity was Amon/Ra/Marduk. In all cases, it means God/Lord, "**who standeth in the congregation of the mighty**," i.e., the twelve gods of the Pantheon of Sumer.

CHAPTER 6

ABRAHAM IN THE SERVICE OF THE GODS

"And Terah lived seventy years, and begat Abram, Nahor, and Haran....And Terah took Abram his son, and Lot the son of Haran his son's son, and Sarai his daughter in law, his son Abram's wife; and they went forth with them from Ur of the Chaldees to go into the land of Canaan; and they came unto Haran, and dwelt there." (*Genesis* 11:26-31).

Counting the generations mentioned in this chapter, we see that Abram was the tenth generation of Noah, the man of the Flood. Beyond that, it offers no answers to the inevitable questions provoked by this chapter such as who was Terah, a patriarch with three sons, two daughters-in-law and a grandson?; why did they leave Ur of the Chaldees to go into the land of Canaan, and why did they changed they mind, settling, instead, in Haran, as the Scripture says? Yet Sumerian texts offer details in abundance on the characters that played key roles in the early history of mankind on Earth, helping us to understand the events and characters who shaped that history, the international relations and great wars during the earliest ages on Earth. The biblical narratives dealing with the beginning of life on Earth, from the emergence of man to Noah and the Flood, Abraham the Patriarch, when Earth was under the rule and influence of the Nephilim, are presented in great detail in Sumerian texts.

From references in the Books of the Prophets, one can learn about the deeds of the Nephilim on Earth, lasting about half a million years since they landed until they left in about 200 B.C.E.,. They report the actions of Yahweh, the chief deity of Sumerian Pantheon: "**God standeth in the congregation of the mighty; he judgeth among the gods**" (*Psalms* 82:1); describe His departure and return: "**The chariot of God - twenty thousand,** (to fit for thousands of angels escorting him)**: the Lord is among them, Sinai the holy.**" (*Psalms* 68:17); and magnificently describe his landing on Sinai, Dilmun, as Prophet Habakkuk did with his golden words:

"God from Teman** (the south) **shall approach, and the Holy One from mount Paran Selah; His glory covered the heavens, and the land is full of his praise; And brightness as light shall be two horns his hands made, and there is the hide of his might; ahead of him goes speech, and sparks extends down his feet. (*Lamentations* (*Habakkuk*) 3:35).

In this regard, one must also refer to the vision presented in *Ezekiel* 1.

So Terah was born in this atmosphere, and moreover, the god remembered Terah's being a descendant of the Lamech lineage, as alluded to in the chapter dealing with the Flood. So, one cannot doubt that the god was partial to that family, whose members were among the ancient Sumerian dignitaries. During the third millennium B.C.E., Third Empire of Ur was at its zenith, ruled by the gods Utu/Shamash and his twin sister Inanna/Ishtar, (the same as Egyptian-Canaanite Ashtoreth), together with their father, Nanar/Sin. A warrior by nature, Inanna managed to expand her sphere of influence as far as Egypt to the west and the Indus plains to the east. Egypt had been under the influence of Amon/Ra/Marduk, her father's cousin. The rivalry between these two families could be traced back to the early ancient Empire of Ur. Now, Inanna successfully seized the Great Pyramid, the center of Marduk's power in Egypt. He was forced to flee northward, all the way to the Black Sea shores, (currently eastern Turkey), where he established the Hittite Kingdom.

Meanwhile, Inanna was watching Marduk's movement with concern, his regional influence, and the preparations he had been making for returning to the center, in Mesopotamia. Her response to this activity was forming a strategic main base, a second Ur, serving as an outpost to check the advance of Marduk. Thus, the temple erected in Haran was designed after the Great Temple of Ur of the Chaldeans. After Terah had moved, with his eldest son named after him, Abram, that is "one whose father is prominent," from the city of Nippur to Ur of the Chaldeans to serve as the high priest of its temple, he was ordered to move on, with his kin, and help start the new center of Haran (see Map A).

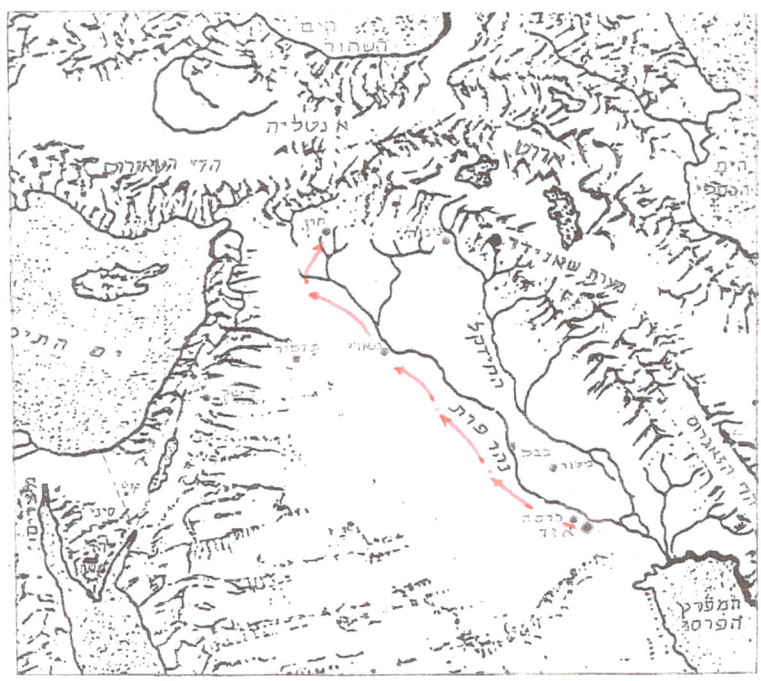

Map A: Terah's travels to Haran

Growing up in Haran, Abram followed his father's footsteps, becoming a sympathizer of the ruling family and their favorites.

"***Now the LORD had said unto Abram: Get thee out of thy country, and from thy homeland, and from thy father's house, unto a land that I will show thee***" (*Genesis* 12:3-5)….. "**[A]nd Abram was seventy and five years old when he departed out of Haran.**" The meager additional information the text offers is that it was Terah who begot Abram, Nahor and Haran. "***And Terah took Abram his son, and Lot the son of Haran his son's son, and Sarai his daughter in law, his son Abram's wife; and they went forth with them from Ur of the Chaldees, to go into the land of Canaan; and they came unto Haran, and dwelt there. And the days of Terah were two hundred and five years; and Terah died in Haran.***" After that, it says that Abram was seventy-five years old when he left Haran to go to Egypt, (2048 B.C.E.).

Who was that Abram that god promised such a great future? Well, we can trace back his family tree: Abram was the tenth generation of Noah, who had lived 300 to 400 years before. Yet Enki, who was, as we have demonstrated,

Noah's relative, lived by a totally different concept of time. As per the latter, it was a matter a few months, so one cannot rule out the significance of kinship through the ages. And a closer look at history as recorded in ancient texts show it to be much more complex. In that era, several gods, who were cousins and nephews branching from the same family tree, interfered in history, each attempting to expand one's domination and influence all over the region and its mortals. Moreover, the gods, whose conflicts deteriorated to all-out wars, recruited mankind to their wars, using them as much as they could. As far as Abram is concerned, he most cleverly used the geostrategic situation, maneuvering between the warring parties, as indicated in the numerous historical texts about that era.

Abram's childhood was spent in the city of Nippur, the religious center of Sumerian and Akkadian Kingdoms, consecrated as the seat of Enlil. Early Sumerian historical texts refer to Terah, who was High Priest of the Temple of Nippur, the highest rank in human hierarchy. Therefore, he named his eldest born in Nippur Ab-ram, that is, "one whose father is prominent." The name "Nippur" comes from Nibbur, or Nibiru, or "traveler"; hence the Hebrew, "a passer-by."

Toward the late third millennium B.C.E., the Third Empire of Ur was expanded significantly, stretching its power all the way to the Indus Valley in the east, and, in the west, increasing its interference in Egypt, especially with the sphere of Inanna's influence (the same as Ishtar/Ashtoreth), Nanar/Sin's daughter and Enlil's granddaughter. Ancient texts frequently report on her travels with her spacecraft mainly referring to the aforementioned seven items of clothing she would wear before a flight, : the **SHUGARRA** (a horned headgear serving for signal transmission); the **chain of small blue stones** worn around her neck (similar to the biblical priestly breastplate), where each stone served for communication at a different frequency; **straps** clasped her breast, fastening a heavy object, probably a parachute; the **pala** *garment* that clothed her body (a pilot's suit), and so on. All these items have something to do with flight, and are always mentioned in texts describing her departure and arrival.

At this time, the center of power shifted to Ur (biblical Ur of the Chaldeans), so Terah moved, with his son, to Ur, to serve in the Great Temple Inanna had erected for her father, god Sin. She also intensified her interference in Egypt, taking over the Pyramids, which became her center of power, and deposed Marduk, son of Enki, who had been the chief deity of Egypt for many years. The latter had to flee from Egypt up north, to Antalya, south of the Caspian Sea. There, in the increasingly stronger Hittite Kingdom, which had gained influence all over the region, Marduk found a new base in an attempt to regain influence and plan his return to the center, Sumer.

Inanna, on her part, didn't sit idly by, establishing Haran as an outpost to check Marduk's influence in the north. There, she also built a great temple modeled after that of Ur. This is the only documented explanation to the travels of Terah and his household to Haran. There, too, he served god Sin and his daughter Inanna as a high priest.

Until the age of 75, Abram lived in Haran, with his father, the high priest of the local temple. A prominent figure in the city, who definitely did well, acquiring a great fortune. Yet his travels didn't stop there. Now, he is ordered to move on: "***Get thee out of thy country (Ur of the Chaldeans), and from thy homeland (Nippur), and from thy father's house.***" Well, this is the lot of a human whose fate is decided by the gods…. "***And Abram took Sarai his wife, and Lot his brother's son, and all their substance that they had gathered, and the souls that they had gotten in Haran; and they went forth to go into the land of Canaan***" (*Genesis*12:5).

Did Abram, with his household, Lot, his brother's son, and all his large train, namely the substance they had gathered and the souls they had gotten in Haran, finally find a safe haven in the land of Canaan? Not a bit! Now, the Bible lists all the places in the land of Canaan that Abram passed through back and forth, starting from Elon Moreh, near Shechem where Yahweh was revealed to him, promising: "***Unto thy seed will I give this land***" (*Genesis*12:7). After building an altar to Yahweh, Abram moves south, to Bethel, invoking Yahweh and building another altar. Then, "***And Abram journeyed, going on still toward the south***" (*Genesis* 12:9), to the Negev. From there he turns westward, all the way to "***[D]own into Egypt to sojourn there; for the famine was grievous in the land***" (ibid., 10).

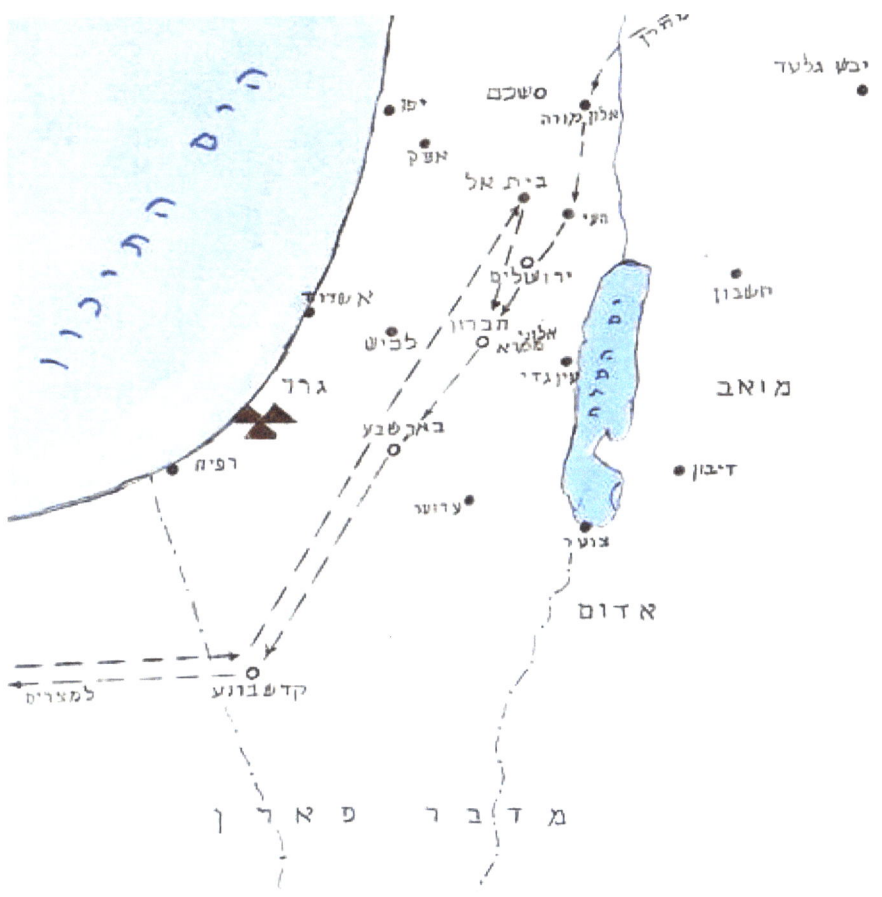

Map B: Abram's Journeys

Yet his journeys were not over and are resumed when Abram comes back from Egypt to the Negev, moving on northward all the way to Bethel, and then back south, until he settled down in Alonei Mamre near Hebron. Here one must be puzzled, wondering what role Abram actually played in all these moves, and to what purpose God ordered him to do so. Was it a part of some grand design beyond human understanding? Since indeed, further developments were unimaginable. Abram's role in this complicated episode would critically affect, for many centuries, the whole of Mesopotamia, and make it the subject of much research to this day.

As the map shows, the travels of Abram back and forth in the land of Canaan were probably in order to be acquainted with the God-promised land, preparing for his future tasks. Abram's journey, in the Bible's words, "*on still towards the south*" was to get him acquainted with the focus of conflicting interests and the major scene of all future events. According to the Bible, Abram came to Egypt and dwelt there; Joseph Ben Matityahu, better known as Josephus Flavius, in his *Against Apion,* says that God mercifully provided for Abram. According to ancient texts, Inanna prepared a proper welcome for Abram in Egypt. The five years he spent in Egypt were dedicated to building and training a formidable army, anticipating the great war about to break. Indeed, as the Bible reports, "**And Abram went up out of Egypt…. into the Negev. And Abram was very rich in cattle, in silver, and in gold**" (*Genesis* 13: 1-2), whatever it took, back then, to run a major war.

In 2048 B.C.E., emotions ran high in the Near East between the families of Sumerian Pantheon gods; a world war was about to break out among the four Mesopotamian kings and five kings of Canaan, one of many conflicts into which the Nephilim drew humans, as reported in *Genesis* 12. Closely examining this chapter, one clearly sees that Inanna commanded the four Mesopotamian kings, while their opponents, five kings of Canaan, were under Marduk's command. According to the Bible, the preparations for this war had begun earlier on, when God addressed Abram in *Genesis* 12: "**Get thee out of thy country, and from thy homeland, and from thy father's house**,… **So Abram departed, as the LORD had spoken unto him…**" and then was God's promise: "**Unto thy seed will I give this land**."

The Bible does not deal with the machinations of Inanna and her father, Sin; as we shall see later on, Marduk's role in the events is beyond the scope of biblical narrative. But before the curtain rises on the major event that was the object of all Abram's moves until he settled down in Hebron, he gets implicated in a conflict presented in the Bible as a war over subordination, among four Sumerian kings against five kings of Canaan who had decided to revolt against them. In the Bible's words: "**And it came to pass in the days of Amraphel king of Shinar, Arioch king of Ellasar, Chedorlaomer king of Elam, and Tidal king of Goyim; That these made war with Bera king of Sodom, and with Birsha king of Gomorrah, Shinab king of Admah, and Shemeber king of Zeboiim, and the king of Bela, which is Zoar. All these were joined together in the vale of Siddim, which is the salt sea. Twelve years they served Chedorlaomer, and in the thirteenth year they rebelled**" (*Genesis*14:1-4).

Before moving forward, one must address some questions the biblical narrative raises so far:

It says that Abram went down to Egypt to dwell there. Right after his arrival, the Bible reports a minor misunderstanding between Abram's wife and Pharaoh, after which Pharaoh sends Abram away with an abundance of presents: "***sheep, and oxen, and he asses, and menservants, and maidservants, and she asses, and camels***" (*Genesis*12:16). Was all that compensation for the minor misunderstanding?

Did Abram actually live in Egypt? If he did, for how long? What became of him there, as well as of all the substance and souls he had taken there with him? The Bible says nothing about that.

Abram came back to the Negev, rich with cattle, silver and gold, etc., why did he go to the Negev once again? The Bible doesn't say he went there to erect an altar and invoke Yahweh. Now, four Sumerian kings declare war on five kings of Canaan. This was no trifle: in addition to the king of Ellasar, or Larsa, which was a city, the other three, namely the kings of Shinar, Elam and Goyim were kings of peoples. On the other hand, the kings of Canaan led a coalition of all the region's cities. Later on the Bible says: "***And in the fourteenth year came Chedorlaomer, and the kings that were with him, and smote the Rephaims in Ashteroth Karnaim, and the Zuzims in Ham, and the Emims in Shaveh Kiriathaim, And the Horites in their mount Seir, unto Elparan, which is by the wilderness. And they returned, and came to Ein mishpat, which is Kadesh, and smote all the country of the Amalekites, and also the Amorites, that dwelt in Hazezon-tamar***" (*Genesis*14:5-7). Well, one must be puzzled at the slaying and total destruction of six nations (could it mean "tribes"?) in the south before the great war which was about to break against the aforementioned kings of Canaan. But all our mysteries are resolved by the Sumerian historical texts dealing with that period, which reveal the active role played by the gods and their conflicting interests. Later on, we shall also be acquainted with the major role Abram played in the great war which is about to break, a world war, by the standards of its time.

Abram was received with great honor in Egypt, after Inanna had given the proper orders. She also made sure to provide him with soldiers, auxiliaries, and weapons, appointing him the commander of that great host. During the five years Abram spend in Egypt, he had been training and preparing his army for the major engagement, the only objective was to seize Kadesh. As the Bible says: "*[A]nd came to Ein mishpat, which is Kadesh.*"

Z. Sitchin

Illustration 10: Top, right: five kings of Canaan headed by Marduk, the figure in the horned helmet. Below: the four Sumerian kings, headed by the figure standing on a horse (probably Amraphel king of Shinar). Opposite them, Abram, riding a horse and guarding the approach to Kadesh Barnea; below it, the crescent and wheat, the icon of Sinai. Left of it is a machine, with wings indicating its flying capability, above it, an eagle ascending.

According to ancient texts, the four Sumerian kings met the five kings of Canaan in Kadesh, the same as Kadesh Barnea. The armies assembled near Kadesh yet never reached it, since Abram had deployed his great army there, together with the five kings of Canaan, as had been prearranged with Marduk/Yahweh; they were to guard Kadesh, a place that was "*kadosh*" (sacred) that is, tightly secured, off limits for mortals. Prophet Habakkuk, who was probably let in, magnificently depicts the landing of Yahweh's spaceship there: "***God from Teman will approach, and the Holy One from mount Paran Selah…***"

He came from Teman, that is, from the south, to land at Kadesh, Dilmun (or Tilmun, land of *til*, Hebrew for "rocket"). It was the massive spaceport of the Nephilim, complete with runways, control tower and communication center. "*Ahead of him goes speech*" and other expressions here describe the landing of the spacecraft of the Nephilim. That strategic maximum-security, closed-to-humans compound was in Sinai, the province of god Sin, Inanna's father, and operated under the control of her brother, Shamash, the god in charge of space flight. This was the ruling family who Abram had been serving.

> The troops commanded by Abram, whose opposing armies faced the gates of Kadesh and that joined the five armies of Canaan, were probably too many for them to handle; so one may assume they withdrew at that time. Later on, according to the Bible, the five kings of Canaan drew the four Sumerian kings south of the Dead Sea where they fought, and were defeated by the Sumerian kings: "[A]*nd the kings of Sodom and Gomorrah fled, and fell there; and they that remained, fled to the mountain*" (*Genesis*14:10).

The Bible also tells us that Abram pursued them, to recover his brother's son, Lot, who had been captured from his residence in Sodom. Sumerian texts report the four defeated Sumerian kings returned to their countries.

> All the while, Marduk had been watching the events; though his alliance was defeated and routed and Kadesh remained untaken thanks to Abram whose massive army secured it. Therefore, it was only appropriate to promote him, the more so since as far as Marduk was concerned, he was not going to just sit on his hands. For him, this was unfinished business, and Abram should be better cared for and prepared for the next phase; "*After these things the word of the LORD came unto Abram in a vision, saying: Fear not, Abram; I am thy shield, and thy exceeding great reward.*" Later in this chapter, we read about the covenant of the pieces that God makes with Abram and God's promise to him: "*Unto thy seed have I given this land from the river of Egypt unto the great river, the river Euphrates*" (*Genesis* 15:18–21).

It had been eleven years since Abram had left Haran for the land of Canaan, and six years since he and his army had held back two armies at the gates of Kadesh Barnea: "*And Abram was fourscore and six years old, when Hagar bare Ishmael to Abram."*(*Genesis*16:16). Though he is blessed with his firstborn, Abram is unhappy, since he is eager to have a son born of his lawfully wedded wife, Sarai. Could God possibly have forgotten him? Or, could this be the promise in the covenant of the pieces. Well, as it turns out, God's time runs at another pace. Another thirteen years pass and Abram was already 99 years old; it had been 24 years since he left Haran, traveling back and forth between Egypt and Canaan, playing a major role in a major regional conflict. Preventing the seizure of Kadesh was a clever tactic, which allowed him a new strategy. Now, Marduk promises Abram: "**Fear not, Abram; I am thy shield, and thy exceeding great reward**."

> Yahweh also remembered how Abram confessed to him one grave concern: his wife, Sarai, was childless, and it's his maid's child who would succeed him. Now God promises once again: "**As for me, behold, my covenant is with thee, and thou shalt be a father of many nations. … As for Sarai thy wife, thou shalt not call her name Sarai, but Sarah shall her name be, And I will bless her, and give thee a son also of her**" (*Genesis* 17:4; 15-16).

Those were the highlights of the Sumerian Kingdom. At 2024 B.C.E., twenty-four years after Abraham left Haran for the land of Canaan, Marduk set his sights on the city of Babel and the Great Temple erected there by Anu, Sumerian chief deity. The steps he took to realize his schemes provoked harsh responses of his opponents, especially the family of Enlil and their descendants, joined by Nergal, Marduk's own brother. Zecharia Sitchin, in a chapter titled "The Nuclear Holocaust" in *The Wars of Gods and Men*, lists the names of gods and their emissaries who led armies of mortals in wars resulted in the destruction of cities and their temples, decimation of their citizens, and massive devastation all over the Kingdom of Ur. At the end of these hostilities among the gods, the Kingdom, too, came to its end; Marduk's rivals decided to defy a unanimous decision of the Assembly of the Gods, betraying the secret location of the "awful, forbidden weapon." So the Destruction of Sodom and Gomorra turned out to be a sideshow. The main objective of destruction was the spaceport and command center hidden at the site of Paramount, and the runways scattered in the near plains. It is from here that Ishum, the same as Ninurta, son of Enlil, set forth to the Paramount, Mount Mashas, or Mount Moses, or Mount St. Catherine, dragging the Seven Menaces; once Ninurta raised his hand, the mountain was shaken and shattered to pieces; straight was turned crooked, and not a single

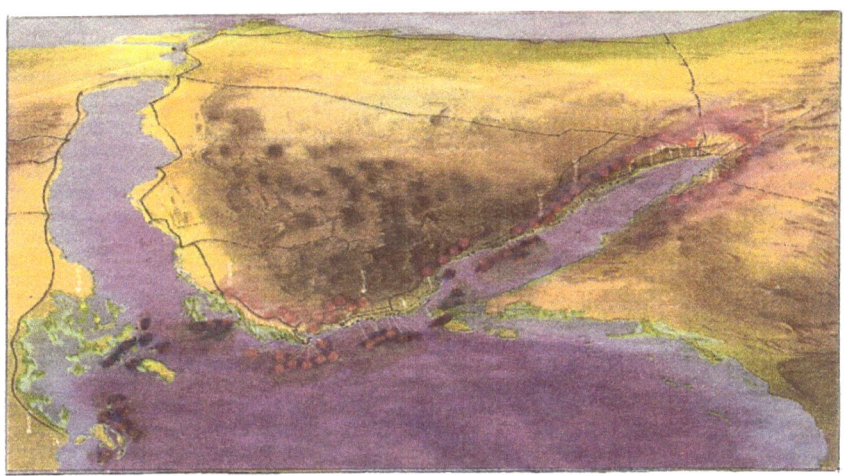

Picture D: The burned surroundings of Mount Moses

tree survived. Thus, the mountain was destroyed with the facilities concealed inside it, the runways obliterated, and control towers in rubble. Dilmun would never look the same.

One can see, to this very day, the mountain and the entire surroundings shining in the burned-brown color of sunshine, as a result of the enormous heat generated by this nuclear explosion, long before Hiroshima and Nagasaki. It started a nuclear tornado, whirling and rising, expanding eastward by the west wind. Sumer itself suffered radioactive contamination, and the gods had to leave Earth. Yet Marduk stayed, operating from Haran. Once the gods returned, Marduk/Yahweh was made the chief of Pantheon. As the *Book of Psalms* put it: "**God standeth in the congregation of the mighty; he judgeth among the gods**," the "congregation of the mighty" being the twelve members of Sumerian Pantheon.

Before the nuclear explosion, Yahweh carefully made sure to get Abraham out of Alonei Mamre, so he relocated to Gerar, on the Mediterranean coast. From now on, the power of all other gods was dwindling, with Marduk becoming the only acting god in historical events and the most influential god in documented history. *Joshua* 24 properly recaps the history of Abraham: "**Your fathers dwelt on the other side of the river in old time, even Terah, the father of Abraham, and the father of Nachor: and they served other gods; And I took your father Abraham from the other side of the river and led him throughout all the land of Canaan**" (*Josh*. 24:2-3). God's promise follows right afterwards: "**Unto thy seed**

will I give this land" (*Genesis*12:7). And Abram was seventy and five years old when he departed out Haran…, under orders of the family of god Sin (see the genealogy of the gods in Chapter 4, Illustration 8).

In *The Twelfth Planet*, Sitchin sets a timeline for the events surrounding the departure of Abraham from Haran for the land of Canaan:

2048 B.C.E.: Abram is 75 years old: "***Get thee out of thy country, and from thy kindred, and from thy father's house***"

2043 B.C.E.: Abram is 80 years old: the War of Four Kings against the Five Kings.

2037 B.C.E.: Abram is 86 years old. Hagar, Abram's maid, bore him a son.

2024 B.C.E.: Abraham is 99 years old. Sumer is destroyed in a nuclear blast.

2023 B.C.E.: Abraham is 100. Sarah, his wife, bore him a son.

CHAPTER 7

DESTRUCTION UPON SUMER

The nuclear blasts in Sinai, Dilmun of the Nephilim, wiped out the runways and other space facilities in the region. Sumer perished, and remained desolate for several millennia. It was neither draught, nor famine, nor thirst, nor Earthquake, as generations of scholars have believed, but the furious actions of the gods that inflicted destruction upon Mesopotamia. Marduk, alerted in advance on the upcoming events, relocated from Babylon to Philistia, away from the pending danger.

Numerous epics, hymns, and lamentations vividly depict the horrors of nuclear disaster resulting in the desolation and abandonment of Sumer. While the gods fled for their lives, the humans, caught in the toxic wind, expired in terrible torments, their bodies piling up on the streets, all animals and plants perished irreversibly. One is shocked to read one of the numerous lamentations depicting, with great anguish, the destruction of Sumer in 2024 B.C.E.:

A Lament to the People

Enlil has abandoned it, the land is bewildered;
Enlil, the prince, abandoned it, the land is bewildered;
The House of E. Share, the House of the city of Nippur
The shrine of E. Kur, the foundation of Enamtila;
He had despised the house of Sippar,
The House of E. Bara and Edikuklamu;
Ha had abandoned the shrine of Babylon
The Esagila, house of Eturkalamu;
He abandoned the shrine of Borsippa
The Temple Ezida, house of Amakhtilu;
The Temple Eteminanka, house of E. Darenu;

In a city damned by its lord,
The queen cries bitterly, uttering a woe, wailing

A city forsaken by its lord
A city Enlil abandoned to the storm.

Its guardian grieves for it.
Its shepherd blows his pipe mournfully.
Its high priest no longer says stop!
Its mourning priest no longer says, calm thy heart!
Its high priest departed from glory,
Its high priest abandoned the Holy of the Holies;
Its lord dwells in it no more;
Its lord cried out furiously, climbed the mountains;
Its queen cried out furiously, climbed the mountains;
The fox bit his own tale;
The pheasant cries out loud;
The reaping storm raged inside it;
The reaping storm raged all around it;
The reaping storm desolated its inside;
The reaping storm desolated all around it;
The house of Nippur is utterly destroyed,
The shrine of E. Kur is utterly destroyed,
The shrine of Babylon is utterly destroyed,
The Esagila was utterly destroyed,
The Temple Ezida was utterly destroyed,
The shrine of Borsippa was utterly destroyed,
The house of Amakhtilu was utterly destroyed,
Eteminanka was utterly destroyed,
E. Darenu was utterly destroyed.

What was the Lord contemplating?
What was his design, in his holy wisdom?
Enlil reduced his land to ruin
The field grows tangled weed
The reaping storm dragged across the Land.
Like a flood storm it completely destroyed the city.
He swept the winds over the black-headed people;
His wife calls him with woeful endless cries;
To our father, Enlil, his wife, Ninlil, cries,
His great lady, ruler of Amach cries out loud:
Oh Enlil! The land is perished!

Oh father Enlil, the land is destroyed!
Oh Enlil!

Wherefore did you lavish your grace upon thy people before,
Forsaking them now?
Why did you assign shepherds to guard their flocks?
Why did you assign shepherds to tend them?
Lord, look after them and have mercy on them.

On October 6, 1945, at 08:45, a tremendous blast shocked the Japanese city of Hiroshima, when an atomic bomb dropped by a U.S. Air Force aircraft took the lives of 100,000 people, leaving countless others injured and sick, many of whom died years later of consequential injuries and contamination. It recurred shortly afterwards, when another Japanese city, Nagasaki, was hit by an atomic bomb.

This tragic end of masses of people bleeding and dying, the devastation caused by the bomb, the horror betrayed by the faces of the dying ones while still alive, the sufferings and torments of slow dying, all these were a mere repetition of what the gods had done when releasing the "awful, forbidden weapon" over Sinai, in the late second millennium, B.C.E.

Plato, referring to it ages later, saying:

"However, they seem, most strangely, to have forgotten the perdition and catastrophic destruction."

Here he probably referred to the nuclear blast carried out by the gods in Dilmun, Sinai, in 2024 B.C.E.

~

Little by little, the gods returned to the region. Marduk, assuming regional domination over and undertaking the restoration of everyday life, was declared chief deity of the Pantheon of the Twelve and remained the dominant and most influential deity until the Nephilim left Earth. Now we can recall the actions preceding the great war triggered by the occupation of the Sinai facilities by the four Sumerian kings, which was the main reason for Marduk staying on Earth after the destruction. We can recall that period and events as depicted in *Genesis* 17-18:

> ***And when Abram was ninety years old and nine, the LORD appeared to Abram, and said unto him, I am the Almighty God; walk before me, and be thou whole hearted; and I will multiply thee exceedingly. As for me, behold, my covenant is with thee, and thou shalt be a father of many nations. Neither shall thy name any more be called Abram, but thy name shall be Abraham; for a father of many nations have I made thee.*** (*Genesis*17: 1, 4-5)

According to our chronology, it's quite reasonable to assume it happened in 2024 B.C.E., and was part of the preparations for the great blast which would inflict a catastrophic destruction on Sumer. The four armies of Shinar returned to their country after failing to seize Dilmun. With the domination of the Second Empire of Ur weakening, on one hand, Marduk's influence grew stronger, already based in Haran, the stronghold of Inanna. It was then that Marduk/Yahweh recalled one special human, without whose substantial help and cooperation, the event might have taken an entirely different course. Definitely, Inanna's welcome of Abram in Egypt, and his being equipped with a massive army for five years was aimed at making him an ally to the four Sumerian kings, and occupy, together with them, the Sinai facilities. Yet Abram foresaw the events, realizing, due to geostrategic considerations, he had better chances of repelling the Sumerian armies, due to the increasing power of Marduk and him joining the five Canaanite armies. Judging from the biblical narrative, one can see there were negotiations with the god making many promises before the major event. However, Abram didn't settle for post-victory promises, but asked the God to give him a son by his wife Sarah. It wasn't long before God responded:

> ***And the LORD appeared unto him in the plains of Mamre: and he sat in the tent open in the heat of the day; And he lift up his eyes and looked, and lo, three***

men stood above him: (Genesis18:1-2); And he said, I will certainly return unto thee within a year; and lo, Sarah thy wife shall have a son (*Genesis*18:10):

Abraham immediately recognized the three men who appeared all of a sudden, as if coming from heaven. One may assume one of them was the deity himself, since later on we read: "*And there came two angels to Sodom*" (*Genesis*19:1).

What about the remaining one? He had to make good on the promise:

"*Sarah thy wife shall bear thee a son indeed; and I will establish my covenant with him for an everlasting covenant, and with his seed after him*" (*Genesis*17:19). He probably came fully equipped to perform a fertilized egg implantation in Sarah's womb. Despite being ninety years old then, too old to give birth, her womb might have been still active and capable of that. Indeed, we read later on: "*And the LORD visited Sarah as he had said, and the LORD did unto Sarah as he had spoken. For Sarah conceived, and bare Abraham a son in his old age, at the set time of which God had spoken to him*" (*Genesis* 21:1).

The two who arrived at Sodom, had a harsh encounter with the wicked sodomites, which was concluded as the Bible says:

"*Then the LORD rained upon Sodom and upon Gomorrah brimstone and fire from the LORD out of heaven; And he overthrew those cities, and all the plain, and all the inhabitants of the cities, and that which grew upon the ground*" (*Genesis* 21:23).

Was it a minor blast preceding the major one? Did Marduk believe he could use it as a threat, preventing the big blast, that of the Seven Awful Ones in Sinai? Only Yahweh knows. At any rate, the Bible refers to this event separately, attributing it to the One and Only God. The return of the Four Kings to their countries, red-faced, after their failed campaign on Kadesh, enhanced the hostility between the families of Inanna and Shamash, making it last for another 19 years. Now the nuclear destruction of 2024 B.C.E. and the catastrophic fate of Sumer following it were inevitable. Probably, the biblical narrative of Sodom was incorporated into the general narrative. The dilemmas raised by its representation in ancient texts can be explained by the constraints of Jewish heritage recorders of attributing all events to one God.

CHAPTER 8

SECRET OF THE PYRAMID

According to the biblical description of the Flood, the Ark was occupied for one year and ten days. Then, the ground started drying up, but there was still water all over the place, with nowhere to go, and no way of gathering any food after the supplies in the Ark had dwindled. The Nephilim sent Noah and his household to planet Nibiru (see the chapter dealing with the Flood), preparing to the restoration of everything destroyed by the Flood; civilization, culture, cities, temples and daily routine established by the Nephilim during the 432,000 years after they had landed on Earth, were reduced to dust as the result of the Flood. To this purpose, they selected seven of their young females to bear human males and another seven to bear human females, to be raised and then help them in their great task. One of the major changes they decided to make was separating themselves from humans, with all the cares for their everyday survival, unsolvable problems, the rapid multiplication of humans, including human females becoming easy prey for the children of Nephilim, (*Genesis* 6). To this purpose, they established the so-called "Royal Cities," ruled by kings, or actually governors, born to them from copulating with the daughters of men, and deemed demigods. Thus, the Nephilim could reside in temples as gods reigning over humans, entrusting the kings, their sons, with everything related to regulating daily life and organizing the labor force necessary for restoring the civilization. Considering mating with daughters of humans, the Nephilim convened the Pantheon Assembly, deciding to ban any contact with them.

One of the most urgent tasks was to rebuild the spaceport in Sinai, or Dilmun, in an expanded design, under the control of god Shamash. Texts unearthed about 160 years ago, refer to this event. When they were first deciphered, Sinai was translated to English as "where the Sun rises and sets." But, following the recent discoveries, a more appropriate translation would be "where Shamash ascends and descends." One can imagine the chief of planning had everything necessary such as detailed maps of the region. So he looked at the summit of Ararat 5500 meters high, covered with permanent snow, seen from afar; the

Land of Canaan, with prominent orientation points such as Mount Zion and the apex of the City of the Sun, Baalbek; the mountain-surrounded Jerusalem and the peak of Mount Moses, currently Saint Catherine, down south, by the bifurcation of the Red Sea. Being a professional, he could look comprehensively, considering all possible ways of enclosing an isosceles-triangular perimeter, serving as a spacecraft-landing zone. This site is actually at very low latitude compared to all the aforementioned locations on the Coastal Plain where the Nile flows into the Mediterranean. But this should not have concerned him, since one can erect a high construction there, visible from afar, against the low altitude of its surroundings (see illustration 11).

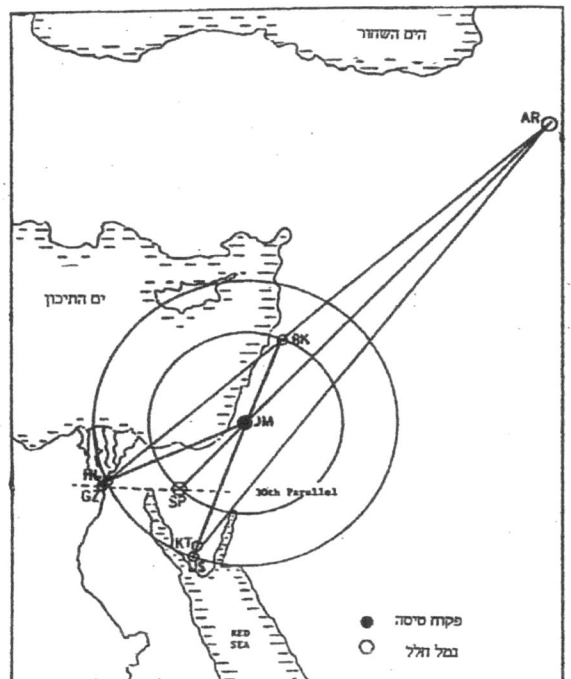

Z. Sitchin

Illustration 11:

Thus, a spacecraft landing strip was formed: the craft, approaching from high altitude, would descend towards Mount Ararat. The distance, from the outer perimeter to Jerusalem, its center, equals the distance between Jerusalem and the two lower points, namely Mount Moses and the Pyramid. The distance between the inner circle and Jerusalem, equals the one between Jerusalem and the landing point in central Sinai, namely Dilmun, near Kadesh Barnea. Jerusalem was the last point before the landing zone. It was from Mount Moriah that landing directions were received; from Mount Zion that orientation points regarding the direction and distance to landing zone were transmitted. We can better understand the significance of this site as a major project of the Nephilim on Earth, if we read once again the splendid description in Habakkuk:

"***A prayer of Habakkuk the prophet…God from Teman shall approach, and the Holy One from mount Paran Selah. His glory covered the heavens***" (*Lamentations* 3:3-6). (See Chapter 6.)

Zechariah Sitchin, in *The Stairway to Heaven*, presents a clay tablet discovered in Sippar, the city of Shamash, depicting the god seated under a canopy, holding a yardstick (see Illustration 12). "***He stood, and measured the Earth***"; opposite him, on the left, are his sister, Ishtar, and his father, Sin, presenting a king holding a pedestal on which rests a large icon of a radiating star, marked with a cross in its center. On top of a palm-tree-shaped pillar, two gods are seen, measuring the pedestal on the ground with a rope. The cross and the radiating heat indicate it is Planet Nibiru.

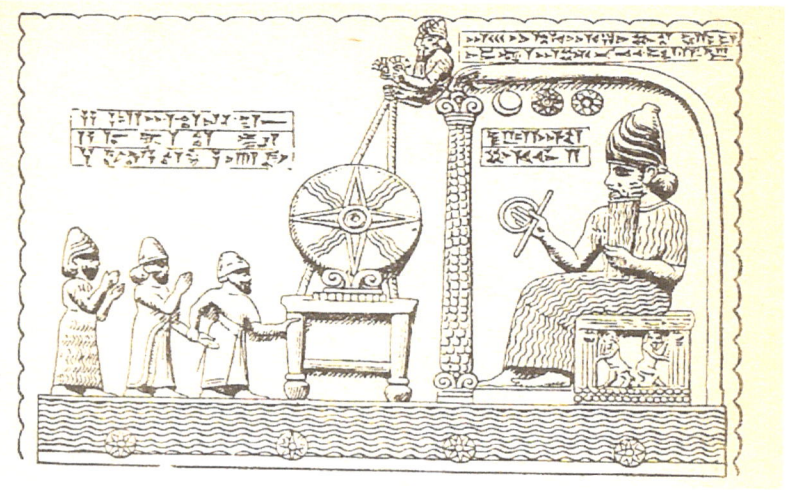

Illustration 12

The three circles above Shamash's head are icons of the Moon-god Sin (left), Nibiru (center), and an eight-horned star, symbolizing Inanna/Ishtar, (see Illustration 4).

There is an astonishing resemblance between the depiction in Habakkuk and the one in the Sippar tablet. It is clearly one of the numerous similarities between biblical texts and the plenty of ancient Near Eastern texts recently discovered and deciphered. The physical evidence still exists in the form of the Ararat Mountains, the magnificent ruins of Heliopolis, or City of the Sun; Kadesh, in Sinai, with the summit of Mount Moses by the sources of rivers; and the Pyramids of Giza, Egypt; let alone the numerous archaeological discoveries confirming the historical narratives, and the great epics on the origins of Life on Earth left by the Anunnaki, or Nephilim, in the great ancient libraries later discovered by archaeologists. Among these is the story of the construction of the Egyptian pyramid, discussed in this chapter. Many pyramids were discovered all over Egypt, scattered in many sites, but none is comparable to the Three Pyramids of Giza, neither by their size, structure, magnificence of visual impression, or the precision to which technology they attest. The Egyptians constructed layer upon layer of pyramids serving to cover their kings' tombs. An attempt to imitate the Pyramid of Giza failed, since it had a 52-degree apex angle. The immense mass of it collapsed, so the later changes of angle formed a sort of twisted pyramid. In addition, unlike the many other pyramids found in Egypt, the Three Pyramids of Giza show no trace of Egyptian civilization or anything to do with Egyptian royal tombs.

The first attempts of constructing a pyramid similar to those of Giza were made by the pharaohs of the Fourth Dynasty. Khufu is reported to have promised to erect a pyramid greater than the one built by his father, the greatest Pyramid of Giza commemorating him for thousands of years. Another two pyramids are named after pharaohs who succeeded him, Khafre and Menkaure. All three pyramids are positioned with great precision in relation to one another, their edges most accurately aligned with the four directions of the compass. It is especially true of the Great Pyramid, which served as an orientation point for construction all over Egypt. It is positioned precisely on Latitude 30 North and is perfectly aligned with its longitude. The proportion of its height to base perimeter is 3.14, the ratio of a circle's radius to its perimeter. The rest of its features, such as its leveled, rectangular base and its extraordinary design, too, indicate a high level of mathematical, geometrical and astronomical knowledge, let alone an administrative capacity of organizing grand-scale construction work.

The middle pyramid, named after Khafre, is slightly smaller: it is 157 meters high, and its base is 236 meters. Yet it was this pyramid that inspired humans' imagination and interest when they saw with amazement such a splendid edifice, which is still considered the largest stone-made construction, surpassing all cathedrals and all other places of worship erected in England since it embraced Christianity.

The outside of the Pyramids was formerly covered with white, smooth Carrera marble plates, making it visible from afar. These heavy slabs were placed next to each other with precision, after being most accurately cut and polished. A mini-pyramid was fitted on the tip of the pyramid, made of stone coated with metal or granite, and removed over time. Only one of those was unearthed, far away, with the following inscription:

The face of king Amen-em-khet is opened,
That he may behold the Lord of the Mountain of Light
When he sails across the sky. (See Illustration 13):

© Z. Sitchin

Illustration 13

Attempts at exploring the inside of the pyramid have been made throughout history, but its descending and ascending passageways were found to be blocked with large rocks preventing further exploration. After great efforts, a large gallery was discovered, leading to what came to be called the Queen's Chamber, with another chamber on top of it, called the King's Chamber. Both of them had solid granite walls, but nothing was found in them to indicate their function. Judging from various texts deciphered over the years, the pyramid served to store everything related to the secrets of regulating daily life, including measures, divine equations, laws and especially standard measurement devices preserved by the permanent temperature inside the pyramid.

Chapter 6, titled "Abraham in the Service of the Gods," speaks about Amon-Ra, chief deity of Egypt, the same as Marduk/Yahweh, referred to by ancient texts when the Pyramid was his stronghold and center of operations, during the Magan civilization, which preceded the Egyptian by over five thousand years.

Ishtar used the long feud between the two Sumerian Pantheon families to take over the entire region, especially Magan, which evolved into Pharaonic Egypt. Accusing Marduk of betraying and operating against the Pantheon in Mesopotamia, she made the gods decide to imprison him in the pyramid. With the help of relatives and assistants, he successfully dug a tunnel all the way down to the pyramid's foundations, escaping. He eventually reached the Black Sea shores, where, according to ancient texts, he established the Hittite Kingdom. Eventually, as reported in Chapter 4, he resumed his position as the chief of the Pantheon of the Twelve. The pyramid, named after Khafre, still stands in Giza, next to its two fellow pyramids, silently attesting to its secret, glorious ancient past.

There was a report written in *Yediot Aharonot*, Israeli daily from the October 11.01.2010, on the Egyptian archaeologist Zahi Hawass' claim that it was not the Israelites who built the Pyramids of Giza. While this is true, the Egyptians incorrectly claim Egyptian laborers to have built the pyramids.

Secret of the Pyramid:

Examining ancient texts, clay tablets, cylinder seals and other artifacts from ancient Sumer, the biblical Shinar, unearthed during the last 160 years, we learn about the Nephilim mentioned in *Genesis* 6. They were super-creatures who landed on Earth about half a million years ago, coming from a recently discovered solar system planet. Here, they established the earliest civilization and culture, currently succeeded by humans.

According to numerous ancient texts and artifacts, the Pyramids of Giza, Egypt, were built by the Nephilim in a land called Magan, after the Flood, which had taken place in 11th Millennium B.C.E., that is, thousands of years before Pharaonic Egypt.

The Great Pyramid named after Khufu was part of a massive Nephilim complex referred to in ancient texts in Dilmun, a logistics center located in Sinai, equipped with spacecraft runways, control towers and telecommunication facilities. It was heavily guarded and off limits to humans. The Giza Pyramid served, among other things, as one point of a triangular landing complex, the apex of which was in Mount Ararat, with its longest side running above Baalbek, the seat of god Shamash, (the same as Heliopolis, or City of the Sun, Shamash being similar to *shemesh*, Hebrew for "sun"). Shamash was in charge of space travel. The other long side of the complex stretched to Mount Moses or Saint Catherine, another high altitude point. Its median line was the landing route, which ran above Jerusalem, or Mount Moriah, where directions regarding the landing in the spaceport were transmitted, near Kadesh Barnea. (See Illustration 11 on page 107.)

Other evidence on the origin of the pyramids not being from Pharaonic Egypt is provided by an ancient illustration deciphered only recently:

© Z. Sitchin

Illustration 14: The Wars of Gods and Men

Segment 1 shows the rectangular base of a triangular structure, with cranes on both sides. The ladders indicate the manner of building.

Segment 2 shows the celebration of the accomplished building and the placing of the apex stone, with a mass feast and beer drinking.

Segment 3 shows the complete pyramid, with a double helix indicating its association with DNA.

All illustrations demonstrate the evident Sumerian traits of the building and figures.

Garden of Secrets   113

© Z. Sitchin

Illustration 15:   Wars of Gods and Men

Another illustration shows a winged pyramid, indicating it association with space travels.

The cross is the icon of Nibiru, an additional solar system planet recently discovered.

CHAPTER 9

THE PRISONER IN THE PYRAMID

Over time, it became an accepted belief that the three Pyramids of Giza, just as the many other pyramids, were built to serve as royal tombs for pharaohs. However, many discovered and deciphered texts, as well as closer looks at the illustrations, tablets and other artifacts dealing with the pyramids, led to the conclusion that the Three Pyramids of Giza actually document the lives and deeds of gods on Earth during pre-Pharaonic times. This new approach allows us to better understand the function of the pyramid named after Khufu, including its inner parts discovered over time, particularly the ascending and descending passageways and the great gallery leading to the chambers called Queen's Chamber and King's Chamber. All these are referred to in detail in Z. Sitchin's *The Wars of God and Men*.

The hostility between the two Pantheon families started earlier on, when mankind started multiplying on Earth (*Genesis* 6). Dependent on the gods for everything, the Black-Headed, as humans were called, disturbed the peace of chief deity Enlil, who declared, alarmed: "**[L]est he put forth his hand, and take also of the tree of life, and eat, and live forever**" (*Genesis* 3:22). Unlike him, his brother, Enki, (the serpent, see Illustration 7) who was deeply engaged in the creation of man, wishing his protégé to grow intelligent, told the woman: "**Ye shall not surely die; For God doth know that in the day ye eat thereof, then your eyes shall be opened, and ye shall be as gods, knowing good and evil.**" (*Genesis* 3:5), Gods, just like humans, suffer sentiments of love, jealousy and hate. Thus, the love affair between Dumuzi, the biblical Tammuz son of Enki and Marduk's older brother, and Inanna, Enlil's granddaughter, started with a hope of reconciliation between the two families, yet ended with tragic revenge, anguish and death. Dumuzi started making moves, planning to become the ruler of Egypt, to the disdain of his brother Marduk. The latter was more concerned on the ambitions of the bride, Inanna. According to ancient texts, Inanna came to visit her fiancée in his province, where the shepherd, Dumuzi, welcomed her. While he was speaking about their future life together, Inanna rushed to him, declaring:

Your Member befits your sweet lips,
Fitting the princely station!
The land rebelled and went oblivious,
I will lead it straight.

I had a vision of a great nation,
Where Dumuzi is god,
Greatly exulted his name, I glorified him

Dumuzi took her in her arms and kisser her, murmuring:

"It is not for servitude that I wed you!
I shall set you a glorious table,
Where you shall sit by my side"

Their wedding was fully attended by friends and relatives of both bride and bridegroom, with an abundant feast and blessings given by grandfather-in-law Enlil and father-in-law Enki, and Inanna's favorite gifts, lapis lazuli pieces. Yet it wasn't long before the feud between the two families restarted, first between brothers, and then extending to all families. According to ancient texts, it was ordered, from the highest authority, to have Dumuzi arrested. Over time, these orders were traced back to Marduk, Inanna's hater. He planned to make Dumuzi the governor of a faraway province, where the couple would be away from the scene of major events. Narrative texts tell us Dumuzi was engaged in many fights, one of which ended with him lethally wounded. Inanna, blaming Marduk for the death of her loved one, decided to fight him in a place called E. Bikh, or "abode of wailing":

Ye paramount, most prominent you are,
Surpassing all....
Your summit is in the highest heavens
I shall wreak destruction on you,
Reducing you to the ground,
Filling your heart with pain and sorrow.

E. Bikh is frequently mentioned in a series of myths referring to the struggle of Inanna with god Ra, who hid inside a mountain, when all she thought of, desired and wished for, was "killing the dragon":

She incessantly beat the sides of E. Bikh,
Hitting all its corners, its heap of stones;
Yet inside…the hidden dragon,
Didn't stop spitting the poison.

That "abode of wailing" was no other than the Great Pyramid. Judging from ancient texts, one may conclude their combat encounter took place in Giza, Egypt. Illustration 16, a Sumerian cylinder seal unearthed in Mesopotamia, depicts Inanna facing Marduk, holding a cup of poison prepared in advance. Marduk is depicted standing above the Three Pyramids of Giza, threatening her with his right hand, while holding an arch in his left hand. The cow's head depicted next to Inanna refers to its nickname in Egypt, "the cow," which was also her icon.

Fig. 73

Illustration 16

The Egyptians continued to worship the cow ages later, as attested by a stanza of the traditional Hanukkah song "Maoz-Zur":

"With sorrow I was exhausted, and much harm I withstood
They embittered my life with hardships, in the Heifer's Kingdom's servitude
Yet He, with His Mighty hand, the Chosen People did redeem
And Pharaoh with his host Sunk like rocks into the deep"

Inanna didn't have to keep fighting, after the gods accepted her demand to keep Marduk entrapped, until his death, inside the Pyramid, or E. Kur, "the mountain house," serving as a prison. For this purpose, they let loose the granite slabs blocking the entrance to the ascending passageways, thus blocking the way out of the chambers. Though Marduk could still roam freely inside, and probably had enough air to breathe, but, having no food or water, he was buried alive, doomed to die slowly. The news of Marduk being locked up reached his son, Nabu, who had quickly found the plans to the passageways from King's Chamber to the bottom of the Pyramid. He gathered several companions to help him in his attempt to get into the Pyramid from its bottom, then working his way upwards, to the blocked point, and from there, boring a passage upwards, reaching the top passageway to the chambers. In the words of ancient texts:

A passage the gods did bore
The lid blocking the passage they removed
Reaching his prison

A short, quick job! The Anunnaki realized the shortest way to get to Marduk would be chiseling a tunnel connecting a passage ascending from the bottom of the pyramid, with a passage running above that one, from the opposite direction, a work that should take just a few hours. While chiseling their way upwards, the Anunnaki reached the granite wall of the King's Chamber. Only the Anunnaki who had built the pyramid had intimate knowledge of the inner design of the great gallery, the King and Queen's Chambers, and the corridors blocking the entrances. Using a little explosive, they managed to breach their way to the King's Chamber, where Marduk was waiting for them. The traces of the blast, dust and rubble piled up on the passageway sides, and the broken stone pieces that fell down to the bottom of the passageways, were discovered by scholars of later periods, and attest to the struggles that took place in the earliest times of the Pyramid, about 2048 B.C.E.

The prisoner had been freed! Mesopotamian texts report him to have gone into exile, and then, the Egyptian god Ra was renamed Amon-Ra, or Ra the Vanished.

Twenty-four years later, he reemerged, moving to resume his deprived rule. Thus, biblical narratives tell us about the devastation of Sodom, Gomorrah, and all settlements in the vicinity, recently confirmed by archaeological excavations. But according to older texts, humanity paid much more dearly for it: a nuclear blast leveled Dilmun, the west wind carrying the nuclear fallout, destroying Sumer.

CHAPTER 10

YAHWEH IS GOD

Sumer, destroyed by the nuclear contamination sweeping it with the western wind, was reduced to wasteland for centuries. The Nephilim left Earth aboard spacecraft moving to Nibiru, which, back then, came close to Earth, orbiting the Sun in a distant elliptical path. The Hittite Pantheon indicates that some Pantheon members stayed on or returned to Earth, to restore the domination of the Twelve.

This rock carving, discovered in the roofless temple of Yazilikaya, modern Eastern Turkey (currently in the Museum of Anatolian civilization, Ankara),

Illustration 17:   A god's embrace

shows Sharruma, a member of Hittite Pantheon, and a Hittite king. Notice the god is seated, while the king stands.

This Pantheon's presence or influence was hardly felt in the region, and only Marduk survived, being way north during the nuclear event in Dilmun. Once the storm calmed, Marduk was proclaimed the chief of the Pantheon, keeping this position until the Anunnaki left Earth, in about 200 B.C.E. This is referred to by *Psalms* 82:1: "**God Standeth in the congregation of the mighty, Among the gods he judgeth.**"

As expected, Marduk returned to the pyramid, and was restored as chief deity during the reign of Amenhotep IV, known as Akhenaton, who abolished all gods but one, declaring that only God exists. Now Marduk had time to rebuild the site destroyed by the nuclear blast in Sinai, restoring the facilities of Dilmun referred to by the Prophet Habakkuk (see Chapter 6, "Abraham in the Service of the Gods"). The Third Kingdom of Ur, starting to decline after the Kadesh fiasco, kept deteriorating and finally ceased to exist. The regional geostrategic changes were manifested by the emergence of small tribes and nations fighting each other over control and influence. Over time, empires such as Akkad, Assyria and Babylon were formed, making their mark on history with campaigns and conquests conducted under the direction of chief deity Marduk, who had different name in each kingdom: A. Shur, as chief Assyrian deity; Bel, as chief Babylonian deity; Ra, as chief Egyptian deity; Yahweh to the Israelites; etc., see Illustration 18.

About 1300 years after the Sinai nuclear blast, Hezekiah reigned over Jerusalem, while Sennacherib reigned over Assyria. For all these years, Yahweh kept his promise to Abraham, Isaac and Jacob, who founded Israel, yet also remembered to punish the Israelites when they seemed to forget or stray from him. A long sequence of rulers served him as a rod to teach Israel a lesson: Tiglath Pileser, between 726 and 722 B.C.E.; Sargon II, between 721 and 705 B.C.E.; Sennacherib, between 704 and 684 B.C.E.; Esarhaddon, between 668 B.C.E. and 627 B.C.E.; and Nebuchadnezzar, from 604 B.C.E. to 562 B.C.E.. Each of them, in turn, inflicted death, destruction and deportation to Mesopotamia. In the words of the Bible: "**On the rivers of Babylon, there we sat down, and there we wept when we remembered Zion**" (*Psalms* 137:1). Finally, in 586 B.C.E., Nebuchadnezzar came, destroying and burning down the First Temple. Of all these, we chose to dwell on the episode of Sennacherib's siege on Jerusalem, since this chapter offers intriguing and significant details on that period in Jewish history, especially on the miracle the Jews experienced in Jerusalem.

These were very hard times, lasting about 500 years, in the history of the Israelites, starting with the death of King Solomon. The Kingdom of Israel was split in two, a northern kingdom named Israel, under Jeroboam, son of Nebat, and a southern kingdom named Judea, under Rehoboam, son of Solomon. While kings rose and fell, fighting each other, both Israel and Judea grew weaker. Kings led hosts against them from the east: Assyrian King Tiglath Pileser conquered Israel, forcing its people into exile; then came Shalmaneser, who brought about another exile; Assyrian King Sennacherib besieged Jerusalem; later on, Esarhaddon and Sardanapalus led campaigns in the region, and then, in 586 B.C.E., Nebuchadnezzar besieged Jerusalem, burning down the First Temple and forcing its citizens into Babylonian exile. Each of these events is an episode in itself, yet, as we said, the episode of Sennacherib's campaign is unique, being documented in detail in both *Book of Kings II* as well as the *Book of Isaiah*. This major event was also documented in ancient Mesopotamian texts free of any religious bias, which offer additional, authentic points of view. Illustration 18 indicates some epithets and names of Yahweh:

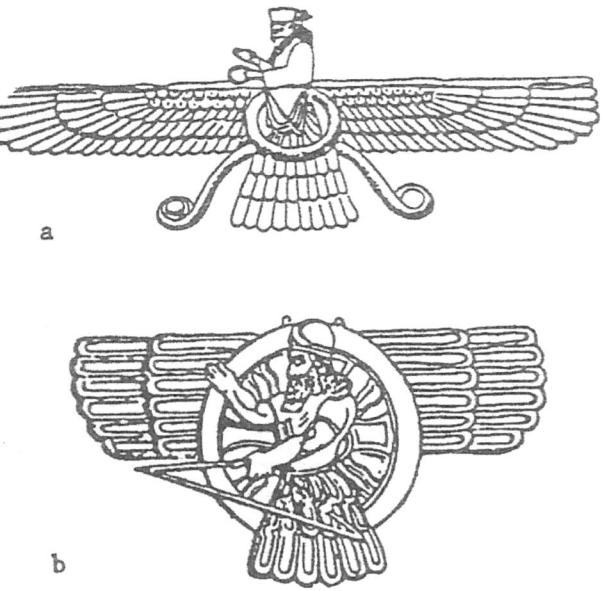

Z. Sitchin

Illustration 18: © The Wars of Gods and Men

Illustration A: Ahura Mazda, Persian God of Light and Truth.

Illustration B: A. Shur, "the Seer," chief Assyrian deity. In Babylon, he was chief deity Bel/Marduk/Lord, the same as Judeo-Christian Yahweh/Jehovah. The winged circle symbolizes planet Nibiru.

According to *Kings II*, 18:13, as well as *Isaiah* 36:1 "**Now in the fourteenth year of king Hezekiah did Sennacherib king of Assyria come up against all the cities of Judah, and took them.**" It happened in about 700 B.C.E.

Sennacherib suffered a very long delay in Lachish, a city situated on a hill, defended by a strong wall. Later on, the Bible says: "**And the king of Assyria sent Rabshakeh from Lachish to Jerusalem unto king Hezekiah with a great army.**" (*Isaiah* 36:2).

By doing this, he sealed his hapless fate, as we shall see later on.

The war was not fought over Jerusalem only; the kings of that time used to go on campaigns aimed at massive territorial conquests and collecting accolades. Steles, that is, monumental stone slabs were found, in which the kings, when back home, reported how they decided to go on a campaign, and their great triumphs over various peoples. In such a stele, discovered by archaeologists in Mesopotamia, Sennacherib wrote he had consulted the god about whether to fight Judea as well, receiving the god's approval but warned to stay away from Jerusalem. He also wrote that the god had promised him assistance in case he ran into trouble. Both biblical and Assyrian narratives do not explain what drove Sennacherib to send Rabshakeh with a great army to Jerusalem, despite the god's warning. Probably, the ongoing siege of Lachish forced him into high expense for an army that fought ineffectively. One may also conclude that Sennacherib was concerned about the mental effect of inaction on his soldiers, and other ill effects. Or, was it the stress of hard fighting that made Sennacherib forget the divine ban?

So Rabshakeh and his army reached Jerusalem, addressing the men on the walls, demanding them to have the king come and listen. Three senior officials came to hear what Rabshakeh told the men standing on the walls: "**Now on whom dost thou trust, that thou rebellest against me? Lo, thou trustest in the staff of this broken reed, on Egypt**" (*Isaiah* 36: 5-6) "**But if thou say to me, We trust in Yahweh our God**" (*Isaiah* 36: 7-10).

"Yahweh said"? Indeed, it was Yahweh, the common regional deity, as we have demonstrated above. More proof of it we can find in the words of the prophets:

"***Behold, I will send and take all the families of the north, saith the LORD, and Nebuchadrezzar the king of Babylon, my servant***" (*Jer.* 25:9);

"***And now have I given all these lands into the hand of Nebuchadnezzar the king of Babylon, my servant***" (*Jer.* 27:6)

"*Behold, I will send Nebuchadnezzar the king of Babylon, my servant*" (*Isaiah* 43:10)

"*Thus saith the LORD to his anointed, to Cyrus, whose right hand I have holden*" (*Isaiah* 45:1)

Rabshakeh refers to Egypt, calling it, "this staff or broken reed." Indeed, this episode shows the god was mad at Hezekiah for negotiating with the king of Egypt preparing a joint attack on the Assyrian army. In the words of the prophets, Isaiah and Jeremiah*:* "*And now what hast thou to do in the way of Egypt, to drink the waters of Sihor?*" (*Jer.* 2:18)

"*Woe to the rebellious children….that go down into Egypt, and have not asked for my word; to strengthen themselves in the strength of Pharaoh, and to trust in the shadow of Egypt!*" (*Jer.* 30:1-2)

The threats made by Rabshakeh were reported to King Hezekiah, who, upon hearing them, tore his clothes, wore a sack and sent Eliakim, the master of his, to Isaiah household, and senior priests, whom they told:

"*And they said unto him, Thus saith Hezekiah, This day is a day of trouble, and of rebuke, and of blasphemy: for the children are come to crisis and there is no strength for birth. It may be Yahweh thy God will hear the words of Rabshakeh…. wherefore lift up thy prayer for the remnant that is left*" (*Isaiah* 37:3-4).

Isaiah, after praying, tells them:

"*Thus shall ye say unto your master, Thus saith the LORD, Be not afraid of the words that thou hast heard, wherewith the servants of the king of Assyria have blasphemed me. Behold, I will send a blast upon him, and he shall hear a rumour, and return to his own land; and I will cause him to fall by the sword in his own land.*"

The rumor spreads indeed, but it takes long for a psychological warfare tactic to take effect, and sometimes it fails. So Rabshakeh keeps making threats, while King Hezekiah prays to Yahweh:

"*Open thine eyes, Yahweh, and see: and hear all the words of Sennacherib, which hath sent to reproach the living God….Now therefore, Yahweh, our God, save us from his hand, that all the kingdoms of the Earth may know that thou art the LORD, even thou only*" (Kings II 19: 16-18).

This time, his prayer is answered. Furthermore, according to what Prophet Isaiah says in the name of Yahweh, one may conclude this time the latter is extremely furious at him:

"*Thus saith Yahweh, God of Israel, Whereas thou hast prayed to me against Sennacherib king of Assyria: This is the word which the LORD hath spoken to him: Whom hast thou reproached and blasphemed? and against whom hast thou exalted thy voice, and lifted up thine eyes on high? even against the Holy One of Israel.....Therefore thus saith the LORD concerning the king of Assyria, He shall not come into this city, nor shoot an arrow there, nor come before it with shields, nor cast a bank against it. By the way that he came, by the same shall he return; Then the angel of the LORD went forth, and smote in the camp of the Assyrians a hundred and fourscore and five thousand: and when they arose early in the morning, behold, they were all dead corpses*" (*Kings II*, 19: 20- 36).

Throughout the narrative, there are no hints to the reasons why Got helped the people of Jerusalem with such a great miracle, while King Hezekiah was negotiating with Egypt, yet Sennacherib should have known Yahweh to be a vengeful god.

The assistance Sennacherib received during his hard-won war on Lachish, as his stele mentions, is hinted at in a relief discovered in Mesopotamia, depicting the siege of Lachish and is currently exhibited in The British Museum. See Illustration 19:

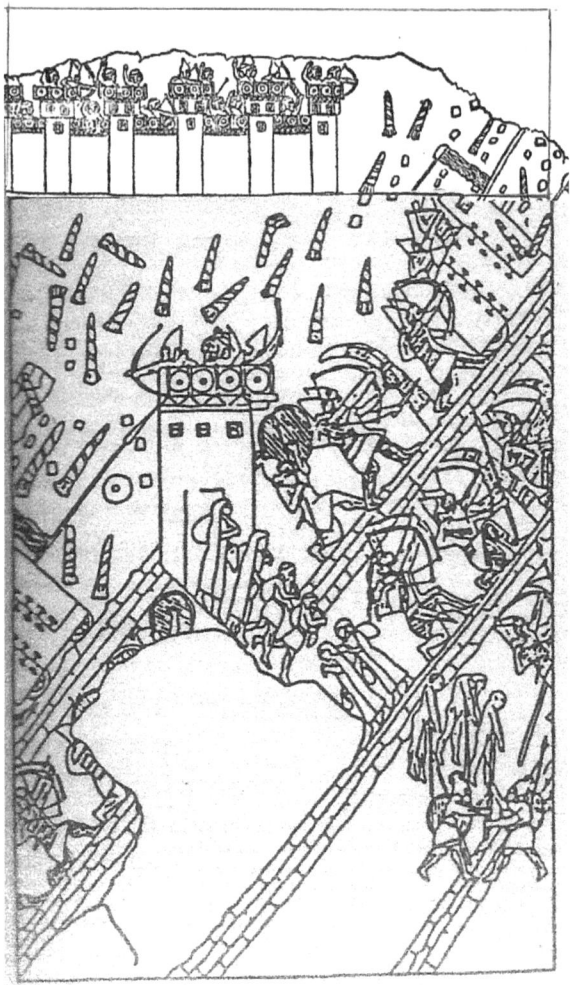

Illustration 19

On the right, we can see the troops of Sennacherib shooting arrows at the city walls. According to the image, the defenders are depicted shooting arrows and throwing torches from the walls. Are these really torches? At a closer look, they seem to be a more advanced technology, and they seem to fly upwards. Thus, the assistance Yahweh promised and lent Sennacherib was probably rockets fired at Lachish, "the shining weapon."

Earth is full of epics and other historical texts, written on clay tablets, documenting fierce wars of the gods with one another, fighting for supreme power. We have already mentioned the ongoing hostilities between the families of Enlil on one hand, and Enki and his son Marduk, on the other hand, expressed in the biblical creation narrative in the form of disputes between Yahweh and the serpent regarding the fate of Adam. Yahweh feared Adam might eat the fruit of the Tree of Knowledge and live forever, while Enki, the serpent, wanted mankind, his minds' child, to grow intelligent.

Over time, there was hope of reconciliation between the feuding families, when Dumuzi, son of Enki, married Inanna, granddaughter of Enlil. But it didn't take long for the hostility between Inanna and Marduk to rekindle, when the War of the Pyramid broke, Inanna scheming to starve Marduk to death, by locking him up inside that most famous monument.

Several years later, the Hittite Kingdom emerged, in the Anatolian Plains, modern Eastern Turkey. Ancient texts tell us that god Tashab's influence spread over all the northern part of ancient Near East. Here, too, many texts refer to age-old wars vying for supremacy. According to one of these texts, Tashab was forced into a burrow until being released by gods who sided with him. In the celestial hand-to-hand combat that god Kumarbi had waged on him, Tashab was armed with "**Thundering Storm shattering rocks into particles**" and with the "**blinding awful lightning**." Such narratives are compatible with those of Sumerian origin. Another narrative deals with a treaty concluded between Hittites and Egyptians following decades of war between these two peoples; it was concluded by marrying the daughter of Hittite King to Pharaoh Ramses II, as was recorded for posterity on a stele. According to the text, Ramses I fell in love with the Hittite princess once he caught sight of her divine beauty, declaring her his queen and saying that "all bounty was given to me by god Ptah." Enki, father of Marduk, regarded as the chief engineer of the Nephilim, spent many efforts on directing the development (*pituah* in Hebrew), and was named "Ptah." Other kings of that time, about three millennia ago, also report on wars they conducted under the protection of Sumerian deities: Assyrian King Tiglet Pileser won a war with the assistance of Nabu, Hadad and Ninurta; Shalmaneser was waging war with weapons provided by Nergal; Sennacherib launched his campaign with the approval of A. Shur-Yahweh; Esarhaddon was fortunate enough to be accompanied by Ishtar-Inanna on his campaign. All these narratives and many more, in the form of epics, other texts and illustrations, written in cuneiform on tablets and cylinder seals, are the offshoots of the Sumerian civilization, which had thrived in the ancient Near East over six millennia ago.

CHAPTER 11

LANDING ON EARTH

When Hittite civilization and history regained scholars' attention, they found another civilization had preceded it, as well as the Egyptian, Assyrian, Babylonian and even Akkadian one, a great civilization which emerged in southern Mesopotamia, that of Sumer. All others were offshoots of what is known to be the first civilization on Earth. Today, we definitely know that it was in Sumer that the first narratives concerning gods and humans were recorded. It is there that many, detailed documents were written regarding the history and prehistory of planet Earth. The discovered ancient monuments, namely pyramids and ziggurats, or stair-shaped Mesopotamian towers, and amazing stone inscriptions would have remained unsolved mysteries if it wasn't for the textual documents offered us to realize the antiquity of these finds, get acquainted with their builders, and find the reasons for their appearance and actions on Earth. The libraries unearthed in the ancient metropolitan centers of Nineveh and Nippur contained edited, numbered and documented tablets written in cuneiform, preserved for millennia from crumbling or tampering. Archives found in other ancient Near Eastern cities had documents sorted by subjects, with their writers names included. When the documents dealt with gods, they were referred to as records of older times, of tablets in an ancient language. Scholars trying to translate them were amazed to read about "ancient cities," "King of Sumer and Akkad" and other kings with their glorious deeds. All these documents mentioned the Sumerians and those preceding them, who had come on board spacecraft, the "gods" who had come from their planet, choosing to settle in southern Mesopotamia, their home away from home. It was called Land of Shomrim, (Hebrew for "watchers"), where the first settlement on Earth started 432 millennia before the Flood. The settlers came from another planet, which the Sumerians considered the twelfth solar-system planet, and just recently discovered. Its orbiting of the Sun takes one *shar*, or 3600 Earth years. It is situated between Mars and Jupiter, crossing the solar system, its name, "the Crossing Planet," or *Nibiru*, in Sumerian, and hence its symbol, the cross.

Ancient texts mention the astronauts' leader, E. A, or "he whose abode is water," who landed on Earth from Nibiru, and, after founding the first city on Earth, Eridu, was renamed En. Ki or "Lord of Earth." As the chief engineer of the Nephilim, he started draining the many marshes on the Persian Gulf coast, in order to develop the area. His major project was developing the mines of Africa, which yielded the gold the Nephilim needed to develop technologies required on their home planet.

Gifted and enterprising by nature Enki won the epithet of *Nudimmud*, or "shaper of things." After he had decided that the gold-production process must be hastened, more Anunnaki were flown to Earth, fifty at a time, supervised by his son, Marduk. One such group of fifty, intended to land on Earth, flew too close to Saturn, a planet with a strong gravitational force, and crashed on it. Maduk quickly reported the disaster to his father:

To the city of Eridu, abode of Enki
To his father, divine Enki,
Rose on a bird, from Dur An Ki
Marduk, from "Babylon" – God's Gateway.

Oh Anu, god of gods; whose world is never defied;
What befell the Anunnaki in Mu, is told to god Anu:
When circling close to Anshar,
The lance toward them was launched.
It has flashed like a fashiond dagger
It has charged forward like death
The sons of gods, Anunnaki 50,
He lowered to the deep of death;
And the flying, birdlike SHUSAR
He has smitten with stormy blast."

Oh, Anu, God of Gods, mighty and awful god!
The Anunnaki who are fifty, he cannot redeem from Anshar.
He shall keep raging forever, and Anshar will live in infamy.

Eridu or "Earth": The first city the Nephilim founded, on the Persian Gulf.

Enki: Marduk's father, the ruler of Western Hemisphere.

Dur. An. Ki: "Bond of heaven and Earth": an epithet of the inner sanctum of Sumerian temples.

Anu: chief deity of the Nephilim, chief of Sumerian Pantheon and ruler of Nibiru.

Anunnaki: The Nephilim who landed on Earth.

Mu: A spacecraft; the same as Shomu in Akkadian and Shem in Western Semitic languages

Anshar: Planet Saturn

Shusar: A spacecraft

Traveling to Earth, the Nephilim came very close to Mars, a planet they were probably acquainted with, especially since taking off to space from Mars is easier than from Earth, due to the former's weaker gravity. Therefore, one may not exclude their landing on Mars for resting, getting equipped and recovering. Indeed, the cylinder stamp, shown in Illustration 20 offers clear proof that the Nephilim had a Martian base:

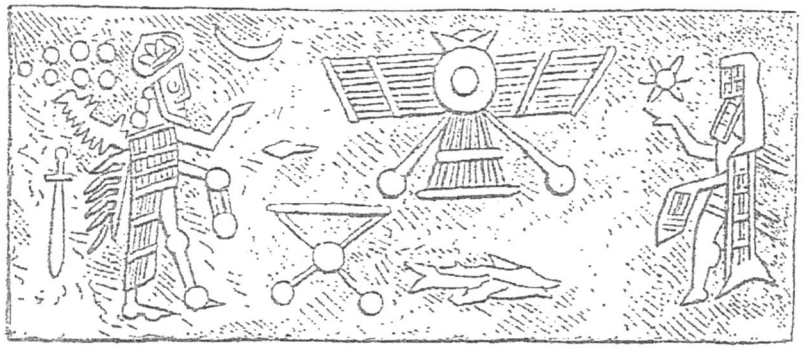

Illustration 20: © Z. Sitchin, The Twelfth Planet

> On the right, we see an astronaut on Mars. He wears a mask, greeting an approaching spacecraft with a gesture. Next to him, there is a six-horned star, indicating Mars, the sixth solar system planet from space.

The figure standing on the left, too, is greeting the spacecraft, shaped like planet Nibiru. Next to this figure, we can see seven circles, indicating Earth, the seventh solar system planet counting from outer space inward.

Over time, more Anunnaki landed on Earth. Some were deployed to help Enki with the mining in Africa, while others worked in the new projects of constructing seven cities in Mesopotamia, in addition to Eridu. According to the master plan of Enlil, each of the cities was designed for a different function of the Nephilim's life on Earth, as their names indicate:

E. Ri. Du: A "house built far away," that is, a home away from home.

La. Ar. Sa: "Watchers of Red Light," was a center of controlling the 300 Iggigi, astronauts traveling in space.

Nippur, or **Nibru**-**Ki** was the "bond of Nibiru and Earth": Nibiru-Earth communication center.

Bad. Tibira: "Where minerals were processed"

La. Ra. Ak: "Watching the blazing light": a landing-direction point.

Sippar, similar to "**Zipor**" (Hebrew for "bird"): A landing site.

Shu. Rup. Pak: A medical care and recuperation center.

Lagash: the eighth of these cities.

Now, the time has come for Anu, ruler of planet Nibiru, to establish the Pantheon of the Twelve on Earth, heading it as the chief deity of the Anunnaki. Now, the ground was also prepared for all the events on Earth for the tens of millennia to come, including the major event of creating the modern humans, or, Homo Sapiens. On the other hand, it also sowed the seeds of future ongoing feuds and struggles between Enki and Enlil, and their descendants, in which Man and his descendants actively participated since the dawn of history until the Nephilim left Earth. These wars were embedded in the human mind and continued in the form of interreligious wars as well as wars over interests and ideologies after the Nephilim had left Earth.

Judging from the half-million years-long activity of the Nephilim, or extraterrestrials on Earth, during which they created man, or Homo Sapiens, by genetically engineering a native creature, one must draw two significant conclusions: 1) There is life outside of Earth; 2) Genes may be combined in several variations, thus creating beings of various levels of intelligence.

The many years of examining ancient texts and illustrations recorded on clay tablets and cylinder seals, which drove me to write this book, confirm the conclusion that "we are not alone," and there is life outside Earth. According to government reports, there were encounters with "little greys," as well as larger ones or their superiors. According to recent reports, there were even remains of alien spacecraft crushed on Earth and alien body parts recovered in several locations and held under guard. One may even go as far as assuming a permanent mental communication between extraterrestrials and humans. The encounters of civilizations with more advanced ones always end up advantageously for the latter and unfortunately for the former. As the former chapters of this book show, this is all about supreme domination. And this goes for the future of this planet, to which we are still bound, since our advanced technology does not allow us yet to escape elsewhere into space, even to our nearest solar system neighbor, namely Mars.

For about two hundred thousand years of their existence, humans were blessed with the presence of extraterrestrials on this planet, both due to their care for humans' wellbeing, as well as to the extraterrestrials using humans for establishing the civilization for which we are its current successors. After they had left Earth, about 2300 years ago, mankind took destiny in its own hands, achieving, in a rather short time, a level of technology capable of impairing the domination of extraterrestrials on Earth, when they come back to our neighborhood. One may only be appalled at the very thought of their response to seeing what humans have done during the several years of their absence: the massive industrial pollution, the demographic overpopulation of millions of humans filling the cities and their vehicles, living in a crowdedness unsustainable for Earth. History tells us such responses had happened before. According to *Genesis* 3:22: "**Then Yahweh the God said,** "**Behold, the man has become like one of us in knowing good and evil. Now, lest he reach out his hand and take also of the tree of life and eat, and live forever**." The Tree of Life offers the knowledge and technological means that allow mankind to escape into space, into the Nephilim time zone, one year lasting 3600 Earth years. But the beginning of that chapter reports the response of another god, called the serpent: "**You will not surely die; For God knows that when you eat of it your eyes will be opened, and you will be like God, knowing good and evil.**" (*Genesis*3: 4-6). While woman feared that eating the fruit of the Tree of Life would result in her death, as man was warned by Yahweh, Enki, the serpent, wanted mankind, his creature, to grow intelligent, gaining knowledge, becoming "***like God, knowing good and evil.***" It is knowledge that allowed mankind to develop technology to allow it, in good time, to start a life outside Earth. About thirteen millennia ago, the gods tried to wipe out mankind. Learning that the Flood was near, they hoped it would deal with the problem, leaving no trace of humans. Upon learning, after the Flood, that Noah and his household had survived, Enlil was furious (see Chapter 5, "The "Flood, Water Upon Earth").

All this leads to the only reasonable conclusion that extraterrestrials possess the technological means to travel to Earth, and they might do this, either in a short time or a few decades from now. But the encounter with them might be traumatic or even fatal for mankind. It may end with humanity being wiped from the face of the Earth to make room for the extraterrestrials who would like to make Earth their comfortable spot, where they could live peacefully, undisturbed by all the troubles related to the existence of humans on this planet.

CONCLUSION

HISTORICAL DOCUMENTATION OVERRULES SCHOLARLY THEORY OR RELIGIOUS DOGMA

About one hundred and fifty years ago, archaeologists started excavating the ruins of Mesopotamia, or the biblical Shinar. Objects found in these excavations, namely various bones, clay tablets, icons, or cylinder seals, written in Akkadian, documented the names of kings and peoples mentioned in the Bible, such as Assyria and Babylon, the contemporaries of Pharaonic Egypt. Further and deeper excavations yielded names unknown to date and documents written in a language unfamiliar and unlike any other known ancient Near Eastern language. Apparently, there was a civilization preceding not just the well-known Roman and Greek ones, but also those discovered later, of Egypt, Assyria and Babylon. That civilization was the earliest on Earth, the Sumerian one, starting at about the sixth millennium B.C.E.

In the northern Mesopotamian city of Nineveh, archaeologists discovered the entire Great Library of Assyrian King Sardanapalus, who ruled from 668 B.C.E. and 627 B.C.E. It contained twenty-five thousand clay tablets categorized by subjects, as well as stone inscriptions, cylinder seals and wall reliefs. A civilized person, and a man of letters, Sardanapalus declared the following, in a tablet placed in the entrance of the library:

> *The god of scribes endowed me with wisdom and taught me the art of writing; I have learned the secret wisdom; to read the words of knowledge, comprehend the secret words engraved in stone,* ABOUT *the days before the Flood.*

Thus he offered us a major source of information on the earliest history of Earth, the "days before the Flood,"—long before it. The library document contained deciphered texts and analyzed artifacts showing, among other things, the Nephilim mentioned in *Genesis* 6. It showed they landed on Earth about half a million years ago; how they created man through genetic engineering about two hundred thousand years after their landing; how the Flood destroyed all the civilization they had created on Earth, and how civilization was restored after the Flood. It was only the Nephilim, beings whose intelligence surpass humans by far, who could have conceived of an epic called *Enuma Elish*, a highly sophisticated account of the formation of the solar system. It is beyond any doubt this epic inspired the biblical creation story, millennia later.

Since its discovery, and due to a poor acquaintance with Sumerian deities, the Enuma Elish creation story has been mistaken for a story about the creation of imagined deities, namely Apsu, god of fresh water, the spouse of Tiamat, salt water goddess; of deities fighting and slaying each other; a story of a knight slaying Tiamat, who was transformed into a monster, and so on.

Chapter 2 of this book deals with it, presenting the full text of Enuma Elish, with an abundance of commentary and evidence explaining our interpretation of the epic. It also tells of the additional, recently discovered solar system planet, which had collided with planet Earth in the beginning of creation, with all the consequences of such a cataclysmic event, about four billion years ago. The epic mentions the emergence of Ilu, or Highest Ones, the Gods of Heaven, the epithet of twelve solar system heavenly bodies. Each of those was associated with one of the Gods of Heaven and Earth, or the Twelve Members of the Sumerian Pantheon, selected from among the Nephilim to dominate Earth for about half a million years until their departure at around 200 B.C.E.

Only the Nephilim could have known about the twelve solar system heavenly bodies, as depicted in cylinder seals and other illustrations. As late as the 19th century, humans knew of only seven planets visible from Earth. In the words of early 20th-century Jewish poet, Bialik:

…seven planets in the skies,
And my mother's Sabbath Eve,
Seven candles, - eyes…

The eighth one, Pluto, was discovered as late as 1930. Together with Earth, they make nine planets. Together with the Sun, the Moon, a planet in the making during the creation, and the recently discovered planet Nibiru, the solar-system heavenly bodies amount to twelve, as accounted for in the Enuma Elish epic. Indeed, modern science confirms what the Nephilim had claimed millennia ago.

The Nephilim are super-beings coming from space, as one may conclude from their description in *Genesis* 6:4: "**The mighty men from the world, men of the Shem.**" "**The world**" means "***universe***," or space, while "***Shem***" is the Akkadian word for spacecraft. The inevitable conclusion is that there is life outside Earth, and we are not alone. The evolution of animals and plants on Earth, too, was a consequence of the planet Nibiru colliding with Earth, as told in the Mesopotamian creation epic, which refers to Tiamat, as "mother of all the living," that is, the only solar system planet where life exists.

One of the major projects of the Nephilim on Earth was the creation of man. Many epics deal with it and other texts discovered by archaeologists, as we have demonstrated throughout this book. According to the biblical creation narrative of *Genesis* 1:26:

> "**Then God said, "Let us make man in our image,**
> **after our likeness…..**
>
> **So God created man in his own image,**
> **In the image of God he created him;**
> **Male and female he created them…**"

Thus, according to the narrative of *Genesis*, man came into being by active creation. Could the Nephilim have known how to make humans? Or maybe the narrative mentions it in three different versions, to demonstrate how difficult it was, and that it cannot be taken literally?

Indeed, the Nephilim were super-beings of intelligence and knowledge, far surpassing our current knowledge. So they were capable of complex genetic engineering and DNA modifications. The creation of man was one of their major feats, which is repeatedly mentioned in ancient texts in detail, since humans appeared on Earth about three hundred millennia ago. The main reason for the creation of mankind was the Nephilim's children resented the hard labor in the mines of Africa. It was reported to Enki, the chief scientific officer of the Nephilim and the one in charge of medicine. Checking all options, he found the solution is out there, roaming in the steppes. It was the result of local evolution, the *ti.it*, or "seed of life" (a word similar to "tit," Hebrew for "clay"). So, it must be infused with the spirit of gods, fitted with the capability of thinking and performing tasks. Thus, one can reconcile creationism with evolutionism: Humans are a result of evolution, an ape, Neanderthal or *Australopithecus afarensis*, upgraded, by the seed of gods, to a higher level, of *Homo Sapiens*.

If so, one must ask, why is there such a difference between the Sumerian concept, which is essentially epic, that is, accurately accounting, reporting and documenting events, and the Jewish, the ethical one, that is, having more to do with faith, rituals and moral and religious doctrine? The scientific examination of human mind had already concluded that religious mentality and the belief in a supreme power result from limited human perception, since humans believe in what they think they know.

Therefore, does God exist? One should rather ask, what kind of god we are talking about, and whether He is the one who created the entire universe, called Yahweh/Lord, who also created man and planted a garden in Eden. To stress the great difference and demonstrate the distance between Yahweh—no matter how superior a being—and the transcendent, inconceivable and unidentifiable God—who has nothing to do with human existence and mind—the kabbalists, formed the theory of *Sefirot*. The Sefirot are levels of wisdom, intelligence and comprehension, as well as other qualities, with imperceptible God on top, and man at the bottom. Above man, yet still at the bottom of the lowest level, one can place the gods, or super-beings, those Twelve Members of the Sumerian Pantheon, who are the Nephilim selected to dominate the Earth (see Illustration 21).

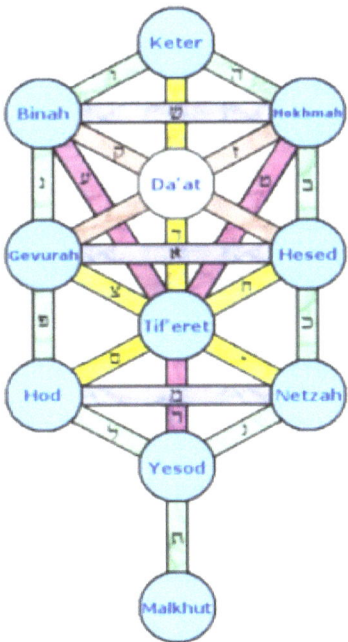

Illustration 21

So what about the Nephilim? Super-beings as they are; what is their concept of a supreme power that created the world? Were they, too, created by a power as superior to them as they are to mankind? How do they deal with the existence of a super-being responsible for the existence of the universe, including their own existence, as super-creatures? Answering these questions is far from easy, but by the very living with gods on Earth, and through examining and interpreting the numerous clay tablets, stone inscriptions, and other artifacts left from the early presence of the Nephilim on Earth, humans can learn a lot about their mindset and concepts.

The Nephilim had no concept of God similar to that of humans. They just believed in the physical world, which for them was more significant than anything else. The appearance of their planet in the terrestrial sky was reason to celebrate. The numerous texts and cylinder-seal illustrations referring to the Nephilim, also repeatedly describe their spacecraft, allowing them to be everywhere on Earth at the same time, as well as the Eagle Men in charge of flying it, under the command of god Shamash, the one in charge of Dilmun and the various facilities of Chariots of the Gods. Illustration 22 shows Eagle Men around the Tree of Life, holding the Bread of Life in their right hands, and carrying the Water of Life in their left hand:

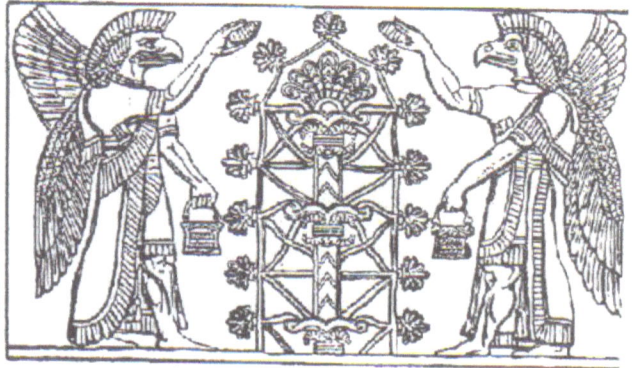

© Z. Sitchin

Illustration 22:   The Twelfth Planet.

One cannot disregard the resemblance of this illustration to the Kabbalistic Sefirot.

EPILOGUE

In 2024 B.C, E., after a bitter, bloody war between two factions of the family of Sumerian gods who ruled the Earth after the Flood, the Nephilim detonated in Dilmum, Sinai, six nuclear devices, "the awful, forbidden weapon." The western wind spread the nuclear fallout, which devastated Sumer and forced the Nephilim into a hasty departure from Earth. It also brought the end to the Third Kingdom of Ur. The only member of Sumerian Pantheon who didn't escape from Earth was Bel\Marduk\Yahweh, who was engaged in empowering the Hittite Kingdom, far north from the nuclear hazard. When the gods returned to Earth, Yahweh was made the chief deity. In the words of *Psalms* 82:2, "**God standeth in the congregation of the mighty**, **judgeth among the gods**." The Congregation of the Mighty is the Pantheon of the twelve Sumerian gods. Since the presence of Nephilim on Earth, Yahweh remained the predominant deity and the only ruler of Earth. The histories of nations emerging after the fall of Sumer, namely Akkadians; Assyrians; Babylonians; Egyptian; Canaanites; Hittites; and so on, the wars between them, and all the geostrategic developments in the region, were directed and influenced by Yahweh.

His association with Abraham the Patriarch started several centuries earlier, ten generations before Abraham, when Enki, father of Marduk, became involved with the family of Lamech, Noah's father. It was Enki who warned Noah of the Flood to come, advising him to build an ark, or vessel. In the war of the four Kings of Shinar against the five kings of Canaan, a world war by contemporary standards, Abraham played a major part. According to *Genesis* 13:14-15: "**Yahweh said to Abram....Lift up your eyes and look from the place where you are, northwards and southwards and eastwards and westwards, for all the land that you see I will give to you and to your offspring forever**." Abram wanders in Canaan, going south to Egypt, and comes back heading a massive army. According to the Bible, the four Kings of Shinar and five kings of Canaan, with their armies, "**turned back and came to En-mishpat** (that is, Kadesh)" (*Genesis* 14:7). Though the armies gathered before Kadesh Barnea, they didn't enter, since Abram, with his massive army, stood in their way (see Illustration 9). Judging from the texts, Abram allied with the five armies of Canaanite kings, under Yahweh, against the four armies of Shinar. The latter came back to Mesopotamia empty-handed, after their major defeat, which resulted in the end of Third Kingdom of Ur.

Abraham made history indeed: he was fortunate to have his descendants settle in Canaan. Since then, the ancestral rights of the Israelites have protected them, not without difficulty, until the Nephilim left Earth in 200 B.C.E. Some dilemmas raised by the biblical narratives can be resolved by the Mesopotamian texts dealing with the great wars of Near Eastern peoples after the Israelite settlement of Canaan. Chapter 10 of this book speaks about the war of Assyrian King Sennacherib on Judea, as documented by Sennacherib himself, offering most instructive information on that period.

During the early 19th century, Europe was swept by the trend of biblical criticism, originating from Germany and carried to Eastern Europe by radical intellectuals expressing heretical views, claiming the biblical narratives to be a historical and distorted; doubting the Bible is a sacred truth and the doctrine of Torah being sacred because of its heavenly origin. Others argued the Pentateuch to be based on several foreign textual sources written thousands of years before the Bible. Jewish Orthodoxy considered such views a threat to Judaism, an assault on the sanctity of the Good Book and an insult to biblical monotheism and the entire Jewish culture. Numerous articles and lectures by many prominent European Jewish religious leaders reduced the effect of this criticism to some extent, but, once archaeologists discovered ancient Mesopotamian texts and artifacts, it regained momentum, culminating with the mid-19th-century publication of critiques by Julius Wellhausen and Friedrich Delitzsch, during the so-called Babel-Bible dispute. Wellhausen, among other things, argued that Israelite culture drew from Mesopotamian sources, while Delitzsch doubted the origin of the Bible and its moral values.

This book cannot dwell on all the bitter responses, developments, and dynamics related to this polemic, or their effects on the European public. But one must bear in mind that Israelite history was marked by recurrent deportations to Assyria, starting from the days of Tiglath Pileser, *circa* 725 B.C.E., followed by Shalmaneser, Sargon and Sennacherib, and then to Babylon, by Esarhaddon, Sardanapalus and Nebuchadnezzar, who destroyed Jerusalem and burned down the First Temple in 586 B.C.E. During their exile, Jews were exposed to numerous cultural texts, surviving from earliest times, especially in the library of Sardanapalus, preserved under the ruins of his palace and discovered about 150 years ago. It makes sense that once the Jews returned to their land, they brought with them what became the sources of inspiration of Jewish doctrine as manifested in Jewish Scripture and the religion evolving out of them during late Patriarchal Age.

Seeing no possibility of continuous denial, Jewish culture decided to respond in the most acceptable way to all nations: namely, that **the Bible was the only document preserving the earliest history of mankind and Earth during the two millennia when the original documents were buried under the ruins of the ancient world.**

B.A. LEVAVI: THE ANCIENT WORLD

HISTORY OF THE EARTH; EARLIEST SETTLEMENT AND CIVILIZATION ON EARTH; WHO WAS YAHWEH

Refutation of Criticism

In July 2012, Eli Eshed's website posted a report commemorating Zecharia Sitchin, who died in October 2010. Eli Eshed is a writer, lecturer, and "culture detective," who had published articles in periodicals and websites on science fiction, comics, and other subjects.

Eshed's article presented many dilemmas concerning Sitchin's theory of the Nephilim, anthropomorphic super-beings, who five hundred millennia ago, landed on Earth, dominating all its events until their departure at about 200 B.C.E.

Receiving the article by e-mail, I saw fit to respond, which resulted in a debate with Eshed copied to his website. His article had two parts, and was concluded with a critical response by Mr. Haim Mazar with several questions addressed to me, "Sitchin's Israeli follower," in his words.

I hereby paraphrase Eshed's post, Haim Mazar's criticism, and my answers to his questions, which may explain the Nephilim and the history of their presence on Earth.

The Twelfth Planet: Part 2

July 20, 2012, by Eli Eshed

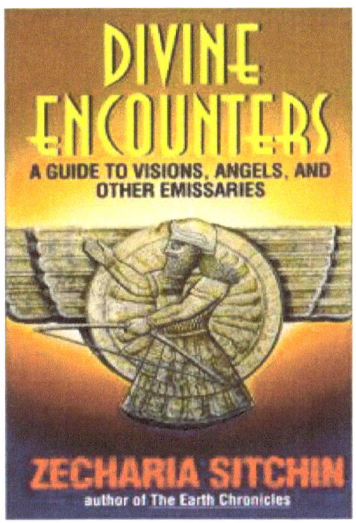

Zecharia Sitchin, when presenting the history of the people of planet Nibiru, the extraterrestrials whom he believed had landed on Earth, and were the inspirations for the deities of the Sumerians, Babylonians, Egyptians, etc., failed to address two questions: 1)Was biblical Yahweh one of these extraterrestrials?; 2) And, when exactly are they expected back?

As I found out, there are serious disagreements on these subjects between Sitchin and his followers who explore and develop the Nibiruan mythology. Some believe the aliens are to return to Earth in 2012, while others offer other dates. Yet one thing is beyond any doubt: in his books, Sitchin just opened the door to many others who started all kinds of mythologies based on the Anunnaki of planet Nibiru. It is yet to be seen what comes out of that door in a few years.

Who of the Anunnaki was God/Lord/Yahveh?

Sitchin, in *Divine Encounters*, compares the biblical god Yahweh and each of the Anunnaki, to find out, once and for all, who of them was God. As we said, Sitchin offers a detailed, intimate description of each Sumerian deity, based on ancient texts, as if he was personally acquainted with them. Quite obviously, he is especially fond of some of them.

Disappointing the readers, who held their breath waiting for the mystery to be solved, he finally reaches the conclusion that none of them had the attributes identical to those of biblical God.

That comparison was probably levelled at his so-called "disciples." For instance, Turnage, to whom we refer later on, claims Moon-god Sin to be no other than the biblical God (*War in Heaven*, p.9). Alan Elford, presenting similar theories in one of his books, identified biblical Yahweh with Sumerian god Ishkur, son of Enlil (*Gods of the New Millennium,* p.362). As we shall see later on, Ben Ami Levavi, Sitchin's Israeli disciple, too, definitely believes Yahweh to be the chief Babylonian deity, Marduk.

Sitchin strongly rules out these arguments, concluding that the biblical God was a cosmic wanderer, probably the same one as Nibiru's god. In other words, the Jews were right all that time: Sumerian deities existed alongside the biblical God, as individual entities.

For the last few years, Sitchin combined his theories with Judeo-Christian doctrines, explaining that the Anunnaki were created by some cosmic being, existing in their own world, and they only served that being. That is to say, the Anunnaki are "angels" rather than "gods."

Garden of Secrets 143

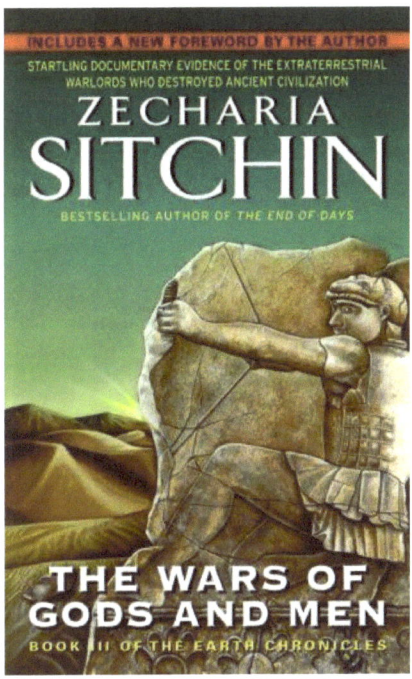

Sitchin's mythology became a great success that no other writer on ancient extraterrestrials on Earth meets with a similar success. The myth he had conceived, (not his ideas only, as in the case of Von Däniken), inspired many others to create, consequently, some "communal universe" based on the history presented in Sitchin's books. This mythology was expanded by other writers, just as any really popular mythology, each contributing his understanding of the planet Nibiru, and some people even claim to communicate with this universe.

One detailed version was that of C. L. Turnage. In her *War in Heaven,* published in 1966 (ff. "Turnage"), she expands the premises of Sitchin to a description of a war waged all over the solar system, destroying Mars, where life had previously existed, and the previously habitable Venus. Sitchin, more modestly, only accounts the war waged on Earth.

Turnage, by the way, identified biblical Yahweh with Sumerian Moon-god Nanar/Sin. Sitchin, in his aforementioned book, categorically rejects this, since Nanar/Sin, as described in Sumerian myths, was already too old and weak during biblical times, to be the intensively active Yahweh. She also predicts, in detail, the events in the End of Times, more precisely, in 2060, when Nibiru comes close to Earth once again, as in the distant past referred to by Sitchin. In that future, the forces of good and evil on Nibiru should fight each other (Turnage, p.19). Actually, these are two opposing political parties. One is the Serpent Party, among whose members are prominent figures such as the god Marduk. A prominent member of the other party is Jesus Christ. These two parties should engage in the final battle on Earth, as prophesied in the Bible. In this battle, a modern Nebuchadnezzar, who Turnage identifies as Saddam Hussein (Turnage, p.86), should play a destructive key role as Marduk's representative, before Jesus Christ, a Nibiruan-human hybrid, should finally come back, leading the Good Nibiruans, destroying the Serpent Party forces, thus realizing all Old and New Testament prophesies. All Christian apocalypse concepts are fully synthesized with Sitcihianism.

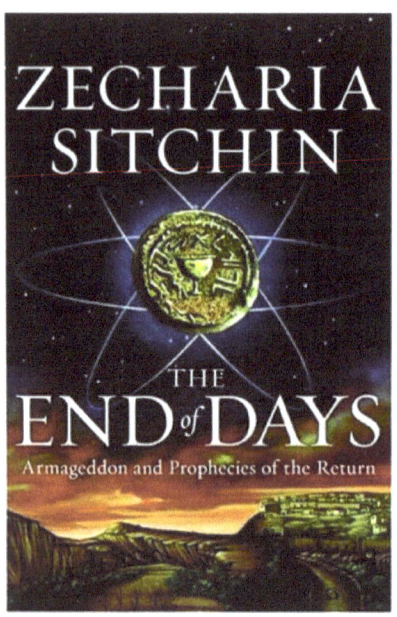

It is difficult to guess what Sitchin would have thought about what others do with his theories, or maybe I should say, "stories." He himself strictly avoided any predictions regarding the time when Nibiru comes once again near Earth, preferring to focus on the past, arguing that the past is the key to the future, and the future has already begun. At any rate, he asserts that the re-approaching Nibiru to Earth is not the same as the End of Days presented in the *Book of Ezekiel* and other prophet accounts. In September 2002, he officially stated he had nothing to do with those predicting Nibiru would come near Earth in 2013.

The alien Bible theory of Sitchin and his followers, invaded popular culture, and its influence can be traced in the popular film and TV series "Stargate," seemingly inspired by Egyptian mythology, but actually takes much from Sitchin's theories, depicting struggles between different races of aliens, who actually inspired the mythologies of the Earth.

In Israel, where all these ideas originated, Sitchin found his follower in Ben Ami Levavi, who has so far translated two of Sitchin's books into Hebrew, and self-published two of his own books where he develops Sitchin's ideas: *Enuma Elish of Shinar* and *Planet Nibiru*, in 2008, and *Secrets of the Bible*: All Mysteries of the Bible Revealed, According to the Kabbalah, Unique Jewish Knowledge.

Sitchin's Israeli follower

However, there is one major difference between Sitchin's and Levavi's theories. Levavi is positive that Yahweh is chief Babylonian deity, Marduk, who still lives somewhere in the solar system, and is probably to return to his primordial terrestrial domain. Unlike him, Sitchin states that Marduk, as well as his son and successor, Nabu, probably died before the reign of Xerxes or maybe before that of Cyrus, somewhere during the last days of the Babylonian Empire. He concludes that, at any rate, they were no longer active during the times of Alexander the Great and probably had left Earth by then.

Ben Ami, in his two books, claims the Kabbalah to be recounting all the Anunnaki tales. I guess this way is as good as any other to clarify Kabbalah secrets, yet a question presents itself. If alien Marduk is the same as the biblical god Yahweh, the creator of the people of Israel proclaiming himself the One and Only God, etc., what practical motive did He have to pay all that attention to the insignificant Near Eastern group, while he should have focused on Babylon, Egypt, and all other places where he was widely recognized as chief, predominant, leading deity, etc., though under various names? What was so special about that little mountain kingdom of Judea, to make Marduk care so much for it, to the extent, as Ben Ami Levavi has it, of seriously hitting the army of his devotee, the most powerful man in the eighth century B.C.E., namely Assyrian King Sennacherib, just to keep him from destroying Jerusalem?

Ben Ami Levavi leaves this question open, offering no plausible explanation.

Garden of Secrets   147

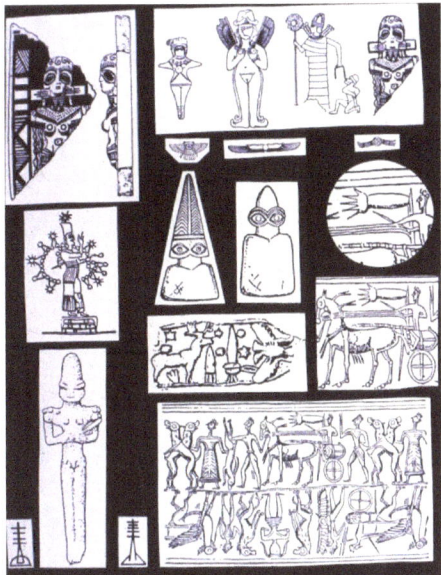

THE EARTH CHRONICLES by ZECHARIA SITCHII

Sitchin's "Gateway to Nibiru."

I'm sorry to say but actually, Sitchin's theory has been disproved, for the last few years, by several Sumerologists who accuse him of misinterpreting or distorting various Sumerian texts. Currently, no serious scholar would approve of his interpretation of Sumerian and Babylonian myths.

Actually, Sitchin created a modern mythology based on ancient ones, regarding the origin of good and evil extraterrestrial beings and the wars between them.

Its believers are positive the Anunnaki will return, as they always do once in several millennia, whenever their planet's orbit comes closer to that of Earth. The only question is when they will return, and what they will do after reappearing on Earth.

Let us just notice that some claim the date of their return to be very near, in 2012. Zecharia Sitchin himself preferred not to specify any dates.

To conclude, here are some books by other writers about Sitchin's Anunnaki and planet Nibiru, each developing them in his own way. I assume that currently, there are at least tens, if not hundreds, of such books, including hundred-page long encyclopedias dealing with the history of the Anunnaki and Nibiru,

Necronomicon-style books of "Mardukite Tradition," synthesizing the ideas of horror writer H. P. Lovecraft with those of Zecharia Sitchin (they are remotely related, to be honest), and probably, there are many others.

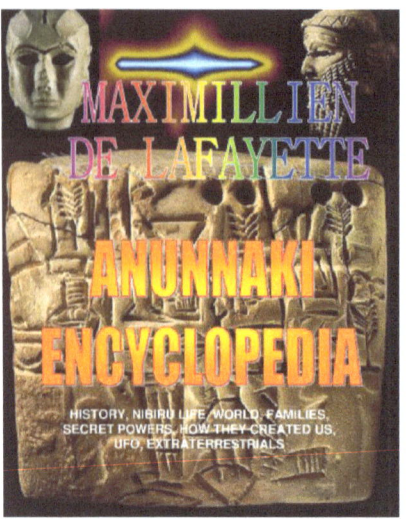

Anunnaki Encyclopedia: History, Nibiru Life, World Powers, Families, Secrets, How They Created Us, Extraterrestrials.

Necronomicon Anunnaki Bible: The Babylonian Mardukite Tradition

Ben Ami Levavi:

The above was Eli Eshed's introductory criticism of Zecharia Sitchin and me, which is presented in its second part. The following several pages contain our correspondence, particularly regarding Eshed's argument that "to what purpose did Marduk-Yahweh privilege the Jews, an insignificant people of no particular importance, over much greater nations and their kings, such as Assyria, Babylon, Egypt and so on?"

To this I replied:

The contacts of the Nephilim with the humans they had created can be traced back to Noah, man of the Flood, when the Nephilim banned their kind from any contact with daughters of men. The only one to have defied this ban was god Enki, said to be intimately related to the family of Lamech, Noah's father. An especially intriguing passage of Scripture in the Qumran Scrolls deals with the conception of Noah. In addition to information on the Watchers, (in Hebrew, "*shomerim*," meaning Sumerians) we read the following on page II of the scrolls:

> "**Behold, I thought in my heart that the conception was of the Watchers, and the pregnancy of the Holy Ones and the Nephilim. Therefore, my heart was moving,** *(from joy to sadness)*, **regarding our infant. So I, Lamech, hastily came to my wife, Bat Enosh, saying: I attest about you by the Supreme One, the Lord and King of All Worlds.**"

And then: "**Noah found favour in the eyes of Yahweh**" (*Genesis* 6:8).

Enki, the serpent, warns Noah about the near Flood.

Ten generations passed between Noah to Abraham, a short while by Nibiruan time, so these relations persevered. As part of it, Abraham played a major part in the war of 2043 B.C.E., when the Nephilim, fighting each other, involved human armies. This way, Abraham had Marduk/Yahweh promoted to the chief of the Pantheon (see Chapter 6- Abraham in service of the Gods).

Following the Sinai nuclear blast, 19 years later, the gods left Earth, except Yahweh, who was engaged, away from the hazard, in establishing the Hittite Kingdom, thus becoming the dominant deity of Earth, making and deposing kings and pitting them against each other, dividing and ruling nations and kings. In the words of the Bible: "***Behold, Yahweh is riding on a swift cloud....And I will stir up Egyptians against Egyptians, and they will fight, each against another, each against his neighbor, a city against city, a kingdom against a kingdom***" (*Isaiah* 19:1-4). For over seven centuries, he has been empowering and weakening more than seven nations, from the Assyrians and Babylonian to the Greeks under Antiochus, the only surviving people throughout history being the Jews. During that period, Jewish texts mention no other gods. When the conditions in Jerusalem grew unbearable, the Prophet, who maintained constant communication with the god, appealed Yahweh in behalf of Hezekiah. "***This day is a day of distress, of rebuke, and of disgrace; children have come to the point of despair, and there is no strength for birth; It may be that the LORD YOUR GOD HEARD ALL THE WORDS OF RABSHAKEH, whom his master the king of Assyria has sent to mock the living God…***"

The Prophet reassures him, time and again: "***Thus Yahweh, the God of Israel: Your prayer to me about Sennacherib king of Assyria I have heard This is the word that Yahweh has spoken concerning him....Whom have you mocked and reviled? Against whom have you raised your voice and lifted your eyes to the heights? Against the Holy One of Israel!***" (*Kings II*, 19). Throughout that page, the harsh words go on and on, and we all know how it ended. If this answer is not sufficient, I don't know what is. I don't think these are commonplace, irrelevant slogans. I find it very important to discuss our history, and see it correctly. If you don't see it this way, I have nothing to say.

The following pages present the critical questions of Haim Mazar, each with my answer to it.

Re: 13:

by Eli Eshed

July 18 2011, 12:17 A.M.

OK.

A comprehensive article by renowned ufologist, Haim Mazar, about Sitchin's ideas, will be published soon.

Twelfth Planet Revisited | Critique on Zecharia Sitchin's Theory

July 20 2011,

By Haim Mazar

Haim Mazar, a member of the Israeli Astronomical Society, is the best known and most appreciated ufologist and alien-expert in Israel. In this article, he offers a profound analysis of the theory of ex-Israeli writer Zecharia Sitchin, currently supported by Israeli writer Ben Ami Levavi, in a series of books claiming all the characters of Sumerian, Babylonian, Assyrian, and even Egyptian mythologies to extraterrestrials from Nibiru, another solar system planet. Or were they? Just how reliable are these claims, based, in turn on Sitchin's acquaintance with Sumerian and Akkadian languages?

This is what Ben Ami Levavi, the Hebrew follower of Zecharia Sitchin, who translated Sitchin's *The Twelfth Planet* (self-published, Herzliya, 2006. Another of Sitchin's books, *Back to Genesis Revisited,* was translated into Hebrew by Esti Oren as early as 1993).

Recently, Ben Ami Levavi has published two original books, namely *Enuma Ekish of Shinar* and *Planet Nibiru: A Historical and Literary Anthology of Ancient Near East* (self-published, 2008), and *Secrets of the Bible: All Mysteries of the Bible Revealed* (self-published, 2010), where he expands Sitchin's theories, focusing on incorporating biblical narratives and the biblical God into the theory of Sitchin, who preferred to base his theory on Sumerian, Babylonian and Egyptian mythologies.

Secrets of Planet Nibiru | My Answers to Mr. Haim Mazar's Questions.

by Ben Ami Levavi.

Right Honorable Haim Mazar threw me quite a challenge in his article on the works of Zecharia Sitchin, may he rest in peace, putting several serious doubts and questions to me, a supporter of Sitchin's theory.

A response to his criticism must be much more extensive that the criticism itself, especially since it involves quotations from several sources, as well as illustrations, since, sometimes, a picture is worth a thousand words. I will try to deal with this important and complex subject as briefly as possible.

In the beginning, Mr. Mazar states:

> "Sitchin's theory, currently supported by Israeli writer Ben Ami Levavi, claims all the characters of Sumerian, Babylonian, Assyrian, and even Egyptian mythologies to extraterrestrials from Nibiru, another solar system planet. Or were they? Just how reliable are these claims, based, in turn on Sitchin's acquaintance with Sumerian and Akkadian languages?"

To this I say that a prowess of language can make you wiser, yet Sitchin, in his books, relies on an ancient epic and other texts, recorded in cuneiform on cylinder seals, stone inscriptions and clay tablets. I, in addition, heavily rely on biblical narratives and the words of the prophets, whenever they confirm ancient Near Eastern texts, as well as the Kabbalah, which is the unique Jewish wisdom. My references to mythologies are only circumstantial or used as additional hints. Neither Sitchin nor I rely on mythologies.

The following are Haim Mazar's questions, each followed by my answer:

Q: These aliens come from a planet, the orbit of which extends to the edge of solar system, a most eccentric orbit. It is covered with total darkness and frozen water, and suffers a long winter. No human-like intelligent life forms can survive there, so how do the extraterrestrials' gold particles protect its atmosphere?

A: Sitchin was aware of that planet's distance from the Sun. In *The Twelfth Planet* he explains that planet Nibiru has an enormous core fusion rate, which heats up the planet's surface and atmosphere. Fearing the dispersion of the planet's atmosphere in space, its inhabitants were forced to place gold plates in space in order to preserve its atmosphere.

Q: Back then, there were few people versed enough in ancient languages to criticize Sitchin. But currently, with the spread of knowledge, many criticize his works, and their criticism, to say the least, is unforgiving.

A: There can be no scientific literature or culture without criticism. However, the big question is how the critics could disregard all the numerous and amazing ancient texts, illustrations and other artifacts discovered by archaeologists for the last 150 years and understood only recently. It is also beyond any doubt that primitive people, in pre-patriarchal ages, were unaware of them. It was only recently, in the wake of technological advances during the last few years, that we realized the magnificence of the Pentateuch, which describes space-travel, telecommunication, distant planets, genetic engineering, extraterrestrials, and so on. Let us look at a brief quote: "**He lifted up his eyes and looked, and behold, three men were standing above him**" (*Genesis*18:2).

He lifted up his eyes, because they appeared out of the blue, landing from above. Well, we know who they were and where they came from. As to whether Sumerian language is fully understood, I cannot tell you definitely. Most of the texts deciphered and translated are from ANEP (*Ancient Near Eastern Pictures Relating to Old Testaments*) and ANET (*Ancient Near Eastern Texts Relating to Old Testament*), edited by Prof. James Pritchard of Princeton. These are anthologies of English translations of texts and pictures deciphered only recently, of Greek sources as well as unearthed Egyptian, Syrian, Hittite, Assyrian Babylonian and other texts referring to Sumerian period.

Q: According to Eli Eshed's article, Sitchin does not make any comparisons with other mythologies, such as Indian or Chinese, and, in the validation of such universal arguments, requires reference to other mythologies. For instance, according to Sitchin, aliens genetically engineered apes in order to create man.

A: Chapter 3, "Gods of Heaven and Earth" of *The Twelfth Planet*, offers a detailed comparison between the concepts of various civilizations regarding the presence of gods on Earth. The Greeks depicted their gods as anthropomorphic.

The illustration above, for instance, depicts the battle between Zeus and Typhon. This is the very same struggle between the chief Sumerian deity

Enlil, and his brother, Enki/E.a ("Ea" meaning "water dweller"). Enki, the chief scientific officer of the Nephilim, was also in charge of medicine, hence his epithet, the serpent. Famously, the serpent is the symbol of medical profession ever since.

© Z. Sitchin, *The Twelfth Planet*. The Sumerian symbol of medicine. The circled cross symbolizes Planet Nibiru.

The Roman name of Typhon was Neptune. In Indian mythology, there is Dyaus\Pitar, the equivalent of Jupiter; Mars, Roman god of war, is the same as Sumerian Lahmu (similar to *"lohem,"* Hebrew for "warrior"), etc. The Vedas, Indian hymns credited to the gods, describe the feuds within the family of gods, just as in the case of the Sumerian Pantheon family. The Hittite civilization, dated back to about 4000 B.C.E., have the same narratives. According to Canaanite mythology, old god El (judging from Illustration 34, it is Marduk) retired, and his son, young Bal, replaced him in running his kingdom. And there are many other examples. All these tales of wars between gods are exactly the same as those about Sumerian gods. It is beyond any doubt that the narratives of various peoples originate from the Sumerians.

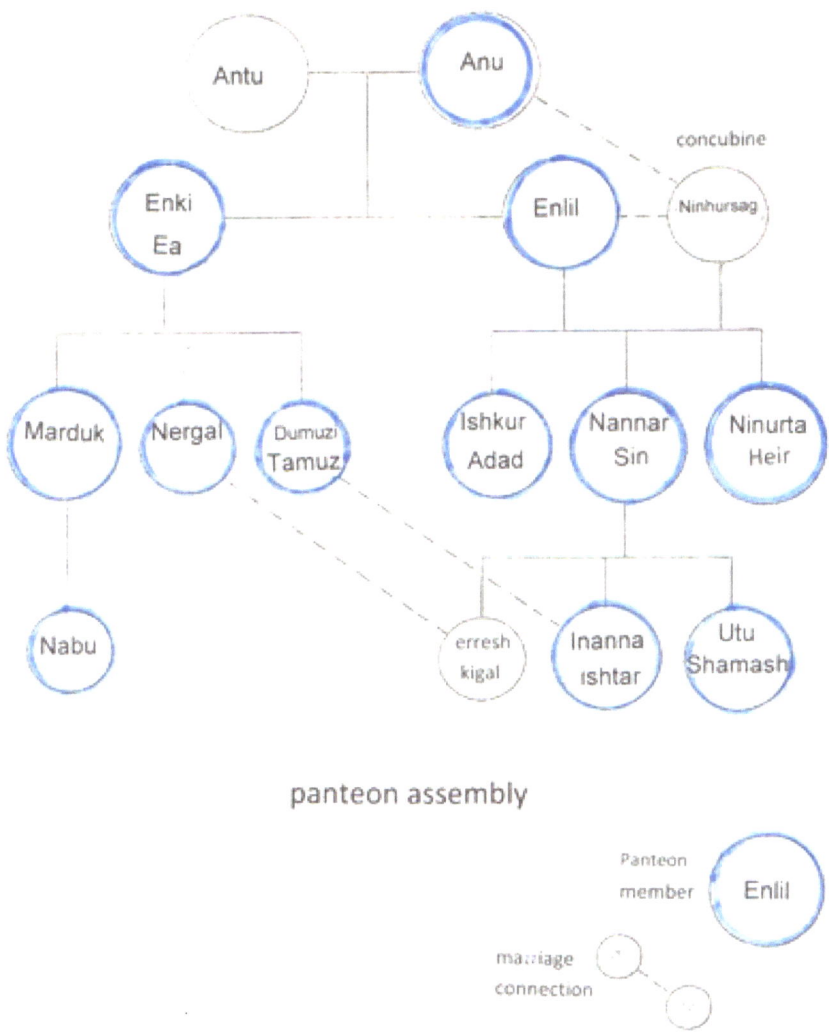

Sumerian Pantheon, the congregation of the mighty.

I don't know of any reference to genetic engineering of apes in Indian mythology. Regarding flying vehicles, similar to Indian Vimanas, the Bible mentions "the strong men of the world, men of Shem," in *Genesis* 6, "*Shem*" being the Akkadian word for "spacecraft." Sumerians knew several types of spacecraft. It is also noteworthy the Muslims had Al-Buraq, the Prophet's flying horse; the Christian had winged people, while the Jews had "***The chariots of God are twenty thousand; thousands of angels; Yahweh is among them; Sinai is holy***" (*Psalms* 68:18). Well, twenty thousand is quite an enormous amount (can it refer to its horsepower?), since it must be capable of driving the thousands of angels escorting the god.

Q: Why isn't a parallel description of such a vehicle, like that of *Ezekiel 1*, mentioned by Sitchin?

A: See Chapter 5, "Rocket-Riding Nephilim," of *The Twelfth Planet*. It deals with the heavenly chariot observed by Prophet Ezekiel. As for the lack of equivalent descriptions of Vimanas in Sumerian mythology and in the anthology *In Those Distant Days* by S. Shifra and Yaakov Klein, it is to be noted that Sitchin does refer to the Vimanas in his works. That anthology contains the story of Enki and Ninmah, the Sumerian version of the creation of man. First goddess, Ninmah, tried to create man as several failed clones. Then Enki told her: "Pour ejaculated semen into a woman's womb, and the woman will give birth to the semen of her womb."

It is beyond doubt the Sumerians knew several types of spacecraft. Goddess Inanna/Ishtar, the same as biblical Ashtoreth, is said to have been equipped with seven items preparing for her journey to visit her sister in the netherworld, i.e., Western Hemisphere. In 1932, archaeologists excavating Mari, discovered a 4000 year old sculpture of the goddess (see illustration below). The seven items were the following:

1. The SHUGARRA she put on her head.
2. "Measuring pendants" on her ears.
3. Chains of small blue stones around her neck.
4. Twin "stones" on her shoulders.
5. A golden cylinder in her hands.
6. **Straps**, clasping her breast.
7. The **PALA garment**, clothed around her body.

"**The SHUGARRA**" (similar to "shigur," or "shidur," Hebrew for "transmission") was a helmet fitted with horns, probably antennas used for transmitting communication.

"***Measuring pendants***," were probably to stabilize her head during take-off.

The chain of stones, or a breastplate, is similar to the one worn by the High Priest in the Tabernacle. It contained 12 stones, serving for communication at different frequencies.

The "***Twin stones***," served to minimize the spacecraft's gravity during climbing.

Garden of Secrets 157

The "***golden cylinder***," judging by its thickness, seems like some device directing the craft in space.

The "***Straps***" served to fasten some object to her back, probably a parachute.

"***The PALA garment***" was certainly a standard pilot's suit.

More images of goddess Inanna/Ishtar/Ashtoreth, famous for being both amorous and warlike.

Q: At any rate, there are no archaeological discoveries even partially confirming Sitchin's claims of alien technologies' presence on Earth in antiquity. Any such discovery would have turned archaeology upside down.

A: Well, seeing is believing:

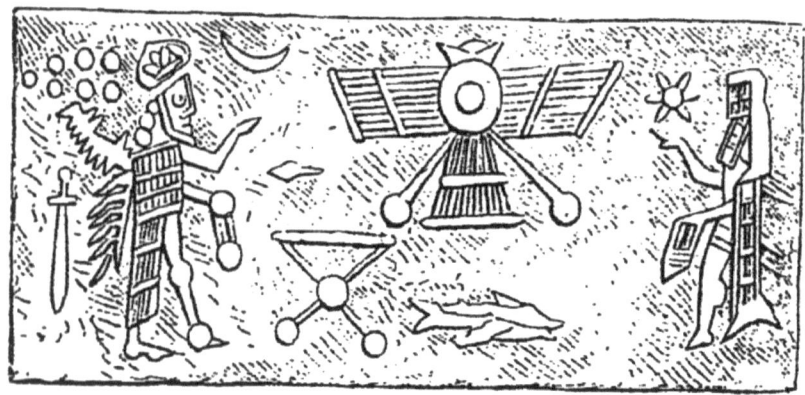

Secrets of the Bible By B. Levavi

The figure on the right is an astronaut on Mars, wearing a face mask. The six-horned star indicates Mars, the sixth planet from out of the solar system.

The figure on the left is on Earth: the seven circles indicate Earth, the seventh planet from outside the system. Both greet the approaching spaceship.

This illustration (No. 9, page 80 in *Secrets of the Bible*), shows a mural discovered in Sinai, in the tomb of an Egyptian official.

It depicts a two-stage rocket, with its upper part above the ground, surrounded by palm trees. Its cylindrical body is inside a silo under the ground, and has several compartments. In the lower compartment, we can see two people; above it, there is a compartment fitted with wheels, and above that, the combustion chamber. The upper part combines a triangle and semicircle, resembling the command module in which Neil Armstrong and his fellow astronauts landed in the ocean after returning from the flight to the Moon.

The following is a headless statuette of an astronaut, in a one-man spacecraft, exhibited in a museum in Turkey.

These above are just a sample of what I have archived.

Q: Any human society has its language and culture, and any intercultural communication involves complicated socialization processes, adaptation problems, and the question of information transforming, so, how did the extraterrestrials delivered information to the Sumerians? Did they know Sumerian, or did the Sumerians know their language?

A: When you have no choice, you adapt. But there is more to it, since this is part of the complex question concerning the various civilizations on Earth, their origins and the reasons for the great versatility of civilizations on such a small planet, especially since today, we are all interrelated and interdependent. But I must focus, referring to the question at face value.

The Nephilim landed on Earth about half a million years ago, starting the first civilizations and culture that humans picked up from them after the Flood, which took place about thirteen millennia ago. The Nephilim started the Sumerian kingdoms after the Flood. The Third Kingdom of Ur we're dealing with was established at about the 5th millennium B.C.E., and ruled by the gods Nanar-Sin and his son, Utu/Shamash, together with his daughter Inanna/Ishtar, twin sister of Shamash. The gods resided in temples controlled by high priests. They communicated with humans through kings, actually governors, of city-states. These were regarded as two-thirds of gods, since they were born to gods married to daughters of men. Noah of the Flood was made the governor of the city of Shuruppak, one of the first cities the Nephilim built after the Flood.

Obviously, they must have had a spoken language or two, but meanwhile, man started populating the Earth, and had daughters, as reported in *Genesis* 6. This meant trouble. Now, the Bible offers us a solution to the language problem: "***Now the whole Earth had one language and the same words…***" Then they said: "***Come, let us build ourselves a city and a tower with its top in the heavens, and let us make a name for ourselves, lest we be dispersed over the face of the whole Earth. So the Lord dispersed them from there over the face of all the Earth, and they left off building the city.***" We all know how it evolved: with human population increasing, conflicts and pressures drive people to form separate groups, thus different nations, outlooks, ways of life, creeds and languages form.

Q: Who wrote the tablets from which Sitchin learned the history of extraterrestrials? Was it the extraterrestrials? Why should they pass on their history? What's in it for them? Is there any evidence to that?

A: The Nephilim documented their history on Earth since their landing to the end of the Third Kingdom of Ur, or Sumer. About 150 years ago, in the city of Nineveh ("***go to Nineveh, the great city***," Yahweh said to Prophet Jonah), a great library of about 25 thousand clay tablets was found, alongside stone inscriptions and other ancient artifacts. King Sardanapalus, who ruled Nineveh from 668 B.C.E. and 627 B.C.E., declared the following, in a tablet placed in the entrance of the library:

"***The god of scripts endowed me with wisdom and taught me the art of writing; I have learned how to read the secrets engraved in stone, comprehend the carved words, about the days before the Flood.***"

"***Before the Flood***" refers hundreds of thousands years of recorded history, preserved by the Nephilim in temples.

A similar library was discovered in the city of Nippur, the city of Abraham.

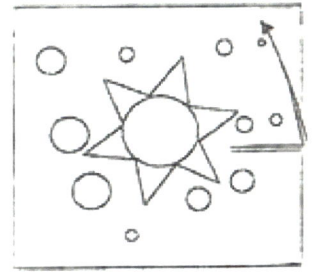 

Mesopotamian cylinder seal shows the solar system between two standing goddesses. A close-up view reveals another planet, between Mars, the small one, and Jupiter, the large one.

Q: Sitchin claims the Nephilim technological advancement is more or less the same as late 20th-century human one. Did it come to a halt?

A: I assume Mr. Mazar is acquainted with human history since Jesus and three monotheistic religions; through Middle Ages; imperialism; the two World Wars and the Holocaust to the birth of Israel. These periods were dark ages in human history in many ways. Great technological breakthroughs only started a few years ago and look where we are; could I have written my books or have made the aforementioned statements fifty years ago? Still, one must understand the Nephilim, who are hundreds of thousands of years old, are by far more advanced than us. In *The Visitors,* Whitley Strieber writes that he had experienced several encounters with extraterrestrials and even communicated with them. He was curious about their energy source: in the spacecraft crashed in Roswell in 1947, no traces of either solid or liquid fuel were found. The answer he received suggests geomagnetic reversal. It is anything but simple, especially since, as far as I can see, it involves rotation. Right now, it sounds like perpetual motion, but I hope human science, within 15 to 25 years, will discover permanent magnetic energy for use in space.

Q: Are these extraterrestrials in some kind of technological Middle Ages?

A: Let's wait until they return, and maybe we could ask them.

Q: Sitchin also claims them to be immortals. A human race can survive for millennia, and even longer, but the basic needs of survival of its individual will eventually drive it to extinction.

A: I have found no claim of immortality in Sitchin's works. I, also, do not claim them to be immortals. Immortality is just an expression meaning "long life." And one must take into consideration that the Nephilim live in a totally different time and space, very different from our concepts of time and time-measurement.

Q: Marc Dem, in *The Lost Tribes from Outer Space,* tries to explain why Jews are the chosen people. Many peoples have similar claims. Do all have similar extraterrestrial background?

A: On this subject, we cannot rely on myths. Abraham was 99 years old when Yahweh was revealed to him in Alonei Mamre. It happened in 2024 B.C.E., when the Nephilim's Kingdom of Ur came to an end. Shortly afterwards, new kingdoms emerged, such as Akkad; Assyria, with its over ten kings; Babylon, with about five kings; and Egypt, with its many pharaohs, as well as several smaller nations. Of all these, only the Jews have survived so far: modern Egyptians are not the same as the Pharaonic ones; modern Iranians are very unlikely to be the Persians of antiquity; Arabs came into being later. So one must ask how do Jews manage? What is their secret?

The Jews' extraterrestrial connection, though, began much earlier: Noah of the Flood was closely associated with god Enki known as "serpent" (see Illustration 7). Ten generations later, the Bible says, "***Terah took Abram his son....and they went forth together from Ur of the Chaldeans to go into the land of Canaan**, but when they came to Haran, they settled there.*"

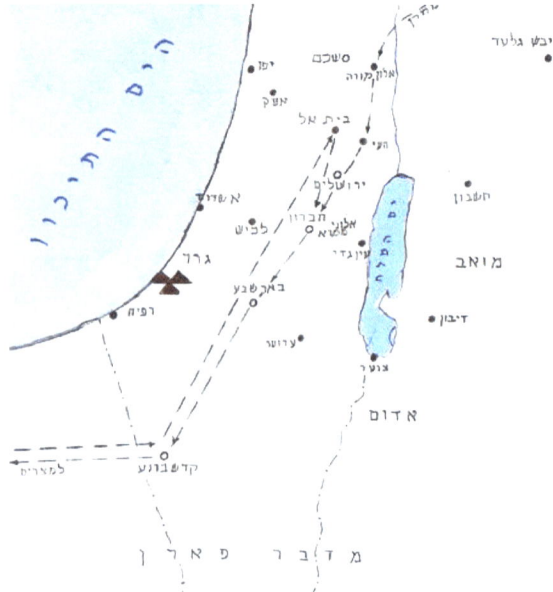

The travels of Abraham in Canaan, to Egypt and back

According to *Genesis*, ten generations passed between Noah to Abraham, and Terah, Abraham's father, was the high priest of the gods' temple. He took his son Abraham and..."*to go into the land of Cnaan*".

"To go into the land of Canaan, but when they came to Haran, they settled there"? The biblical narratives did not specify their motive, or what business they had being in Haran, but ancient Mesopotamian texts are full of episodes involving our ancestors, of which we had no idea. So actually, Terah was sent to Haran, to build a city and a temple similar to that of Ur, as an outpost of Ishtar and her brother against Marduk, who they forced out of the Pyramids of Egypt. Marduk, the same as Egyptian Amon-Ra, after he had started the Hittite Kingdom, was plotting his return to Sumer.

The Nephilim had no army of their own, so they carefully raised human armies, thus involving humans in their feuds. Thus, Abraham was sent to Egypt in 2048 B.C.E., where Ishtar carefully equipped him with a massive army, anticipating the great war of four Sumerian kings against the five Canaanite kings under Marduk (*Genesis* 14). Their objective was seizing Dilmun, a spaceport with runways, control towers and other facilities in Sinai, controlled by god Shamash.

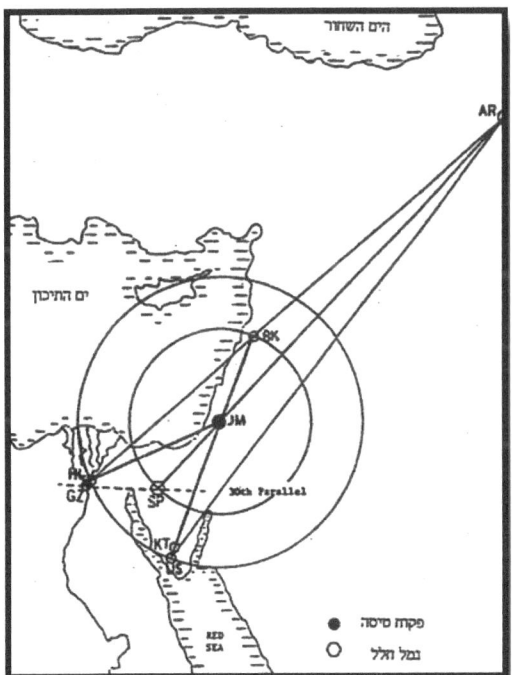

It was called Kadesh, or "Kadesh Bar-nea," a guarded perimeter, off limits for humans.

"***Then they turned back and came to En-mishpat*** (that is, Kadesh)" (*Genesis*14:7). The four armies gathered near the place but didn't get there, since Abram, with his army, blocked their way:

Z. Sitchin, *The 12th Planet*

Top right: five Canaanite armies, headed by Marduk, recognized by his horned headgear.

Bottom: Four Sumerian armies, headed by the figure standing on a horseback. Opposite them, Abram guarding the entrance of Kadesh, symbolized by a technological device with wings, indicating its flight capability. Above it, we can see two persons greeting an eagle taking off. The astronaut flying the craft was referred as "Eagle."

Genesis 12 indicates that some promises were given to Abram even before the Sinai encounter: "***Go from your country and your kindred and your father's house to the land that I will show you.***" I believe Yahweh planned in advance to start a nation faithful to him and serving as the Lamp of Nations, as attested by the later appearance of the Ten Commandments and Hammurabi's Laws. I found the best manifestation of the god's attitude in *Kings II*:18 and *Isaiah* 36, reporting the campaign of Assyrian king Sennacherib in Jerusalem. Before going on his campaign in Canaan, Sennacherib consulted god A. Shur/Lord Yahweh, who promised his assistance, but warned him to stay away from Jerusalem. Defying the god's warning, Sennacherib sent Rabshakeh, with a massive army to besiege the city. When the condition of the city grew unbearable, Prophet Isaiah was told by King Hezekiah to explain to Yahweh how serious the situation was. After praying, Isaiah says: "***This is the word which Yahweh hath spoken to him: Whom hast thou reproached and blasphemed? and against whom hast thou exalted thy voice, and lifted up thine eyes on high? even against the Holy One of Israel***" (Kings II 19:20).... going on, using harsh words, and we all know how this episode ended.

Q: When meeting with Mr. Ben Ami Levavi, the Israeli follower of Zecharia Sitchin, he pointed out to me a passage in *Habakkuk* 3, which reads "***Ahead of him goes speech, and sparks shoot down his feet***." He believed "spark" can only refer to the flames bursting out of a rocket's exhaust nozzles. This is a very far-fetched interpretation, since this passage has no technical descriptions, as opposed to *Ezekiel I*. Although this verse was just a part of what Levavi said, I have my reservation regarding his approach.

A: Well, everyone has his preferences. Haim Mazar prefers the technical specifications of Ezekiel. Speaking to that point, Mazar only takes one verse from Habakkuk, which doesn't mean much. Habakkuk actually visited that site, it is better to read his splendid description, in grand biblical vocabulary, of the astonishing site of spacecraft landing. Unlike Ezekiel, who offers technical specifications of the chariot, Habakkuk expresses his innocent admiration of the god's appearance:

"***God from the south shall approach, and the Holy One from mount Paran Selah. His glory covered the heavens, and the Earth was full of his praise. And his brightness was as the light like two horns his hands made, and there is the hide of his might. Ahead of him goes speech, and sparks shoot down his feet. He stood, and measured the Earth***" (Hab. 3:3-6).

This is an accurate description of a spacecraft's approach. Ancient people, watching this "planet" coming, assumed it to be Jupiter, but it moves from east to west, not from the south, unlike the direction all planets move. The spacecraft, approaching from high altitude, makes a wide circle, heading for Ararat Mountain, its first orientation point: a 5500-meter altitude, covered with permanent snow. Then it turns towards Jerusalem, preparing to land in Dilmun.

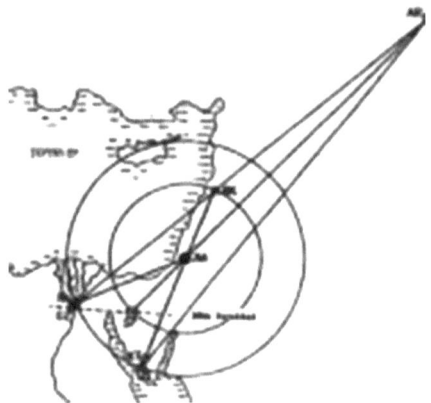

The Twelfth Planet by Z. Sitchin

The triangular landing perimeter, with the top vertex on Ararat, the bottom one on Mount Moses (Saint Catherine) and the third on the Pyramid of Giza.

Q: It raises many questions and dilemmas. The main question is whether Sitchin and his followers have any scientific or engineering background, since any ignorance in these fields may lead to conclusion with no scientific grounds.

A: I cannot see how it is relevant! Is it sciences and engineering we're dealing with? And who is meant by "Sitchin and his followers"? As far as I, Ben Ami Levavi, am concerned, I hate to talk about myself, but you left me no choice. The Bible has been my companion since childhood, to this very day. When I was young, I studied engineering at the Institution of Engineering and Technology, UK, and as a young man, I worked on low voltage and high-voltage power line design. Later, I started and directed an engineering and development company, and was intensively engaged in helping build Israel. I am very sorry for having to state all that, since I adhere to not blowing one's own horn. So Haim Mazar got the impression that Sitchin fashioned, out of Sumerian mythology, a new one.

To conclude:

Zecharia Sitchin, may he rest in peace, wrote several books about earliest human history, which were published in numerous countries, but not in Israel, profoundly shaking our concepts on the subjects prevailing until a few years ago. Closely reading the many questions and my answers to them, one may conclude that Zechariah Sitchin had done a most comprehensive and thorough work, supporting his arguments with much textual evidence, illustrations and photos, of cylinder seals and many other relevant items.

INDEX

Akkad – 8, 13, 15, 17, 25, 27, 37, 65, 68, 69, 73, 74, 86, 91, 119, 126, 128, 132, 134, 137, 151, 152, 155, 162

Amon-Ra - 71, 87, 89, 110, 117, 163

Anshar – 7, 18, 19, 21, 23, 25, 26, 27-35, 37, 38, 42, 45, 48, 50, 55, 72, 127, 128

Anu – 7, 18, 19, 21, 24, 25, 28-30, 36, 37, 40, 42-45, 47-49, 52, 53, 56, 57, 67, 69, 73, 98, 127-129

Anunnaki – 2, 24, 28, 36, 40, 56-59, 73, 109, 117, 119, 127-129, 141, 142, 146-148

A. Shur – 119, 120, 125, 164

Assyria – 3, 6, 66, 74, 75, 87, 119-123, 125, 126, 132, 137, 138, 146, 149-153, 162, 164,

Asteroid belt – 6, 9-12, 53, 81

Babylon, Babel – 3, 5, 6, 10, 11, 15, 27, 31, 43, 49, 53, 55, 58, 59, 66, 68, 71, 74, 75, 87, 98, 101, 102, 119-122, 126, 127, 132, 137, 138, 141, 142, 146-153, 162

Ben Zoma – 1

Ben Uzai - 1

Celestial Battle – 5, 6, 11, 14, 15, 43, 49, 53, 57, 73

Cylinder seal – 1-3, 10, 11, 14, 111, 116, 125, 129, 132, 133, 136, 152, 161, 166

Dilmun – 68, 80, 81, 89, 96, 99, 101, 103, 104, 106, 108, 111, 117, 119, 136, 163, 165

Duggae - 51

Dumuzi-Tammuz – 73, 114, 115, 125

Dur. An. Ki – 127,

Earth – 2-15, 18, 19, 21, 23, 25, 41, 43, 47, 49, 51, 53, 56, 57, 59-75, 77-79, 81, 83-86, 99, 101, 104, 106, 108-111, 114, 116, 118, 119, 122, 125-141, 143-147, 150, 153, 157-160, 165

E. Bikh - 115

E. Din – 69, 70

E. Kur – 101, 102, 116

Elisha, Ben Abuyah - 1

Enki – 2, 7, 19, 25, 49, 61, 66, 67, 69-74, 78, 85, 86, 90, 91, 114, 115, 125, 127-130, 134, 137, 149, 154, 156, 162

Enlil – 7, 49, 52, 53, 58, 65, 67, 69, 70, 72, 73, 81, 82, 86, 91, 98, 101-103, 114, 115, 125, 129, 130, 142, 154

Enuma Elish – 2-4, 6-9, 11, 13-15, 17, 27, 41, 60, 70, 73, 87, 133, 145

E. Share -101

Flood – 2-4, 12, 13, 46, 48, 49, 65, 66, 69-71, 73, 77-79, 83-86, 88, 89, 101, 102, 106, 111, 126, 130, 132, 133, 137, 149, 159, 160, 162

Gaga- 7, 32-37, 41, 45, 55, 73
Gilgamesh – 2, 79-83, 86

Haran- 59, 88-90, 92, 97-100, 104, 162, 163

Igigi – 40, 41, 56, 57
Inanna – 68, 69, 71-74, 78, 89, 91, 92, 94, 96, 97, 104, 105, 108, 114-116, 125, 156, 157, 160
Ishkur-Hadad – 7, 69, 125, 142

Kadesh Bar-Nea – 81,95-98, 105, 108, 109, 112, 119, 137, 164
Kingu – 7, 14, 24-29, 34-38, 40, 46-51, 53, 56, 57, 73, 79
Kishar – 7, 18, 19, 25, 33, 37, 45, 53, 72

Lahamu – 5, 7, 18, 19, 25, 29, 32, 36, 37, 38, 40, 51, 53, 71
Lahmu – 5, 7, 18, 19, 25, 32, 36, 37, 40, 41, 51, 53, 71, 154
Layard, Henry Austen – 12

Marduk – 5-7, 10-12, 15, 29-33, 35-37, 40-45, 47-51, 53-60, 66, 70-72, 74, 87, 89, 91, 92, 94, 96-99, 101, 104, 105, 110, 111, 114-117, 119, 120, 125, 127, 137, 142, 144, 146, 148-150, 154, 163, 164
Mercury – 5, 7, 9, 10, 19, 21, 68, 71
Mummu – 5, 7, 18-23, 25, 27-29, 68

Nanar-Sin – 7, 49, 68, 73, 89, 91, 143, 160
Nephilim – 2, 3, 4, 37, 41, 57, 63-65, 69, 70, 73-75, 77-79, 81, 84, 88, 94, 97, 101, 104, 106, 108, 109, 111, 118, 125, 127-130, 132-138, 140, 149, 154, 156, 159-163
Nergal – 7, 72, 98, 125
Nibiru – 2, 3, 5-7, 10-13, 15, 29, 31, 33, 35, 37, 43, 47, 52, 53, 55, 59, 60, 67, 69, 70, 73, 74, 78, 79, 81, 83, 84, 106, 108, 113, 118, 120, 126-129, 133, 134, 141-145, 147-149, 151, 152, 154
Nudimmud – 7, 18, 19, 21, 25, 33, 36, 37, 40, 45, 50, 52, 57, 73, 127

PARDES – 1
Protector- 23
Ptah – 125

Sardanapalus – 4, 12, 132, 138, 160
Serpent -22, 23, 26, 34, 38, 65, 66, 70, 73, 84, 114, 125, 130, 144, 149, 154, 162
Shamash – 68, 71, 74, 79, 81, 89, 97, 105, 106, 108, 111, 136, 160, 163
Shem – 64, 65, 68, 79-81, 84, 94, 111, 128, 134, 155
Shinar – 1, 12-14, 60, 78, 81, 84, 94-96, 104, 111, 132, 137, 138, 145, 151
Sin – 7, 25, 29,49, 51, 68, 69, 71, 73, 74, 79, 89, 91, 92, 94, 97, 100, 108, 142, 143, 160
Sitchin – 10, 13, 31, 33, 66, 74, 79, 80, 96, 98, 100, 107, 108, 110, 112, 113, 114, 120, 128, 136, 140, 141-149, 151-154, 156, 157, 160-162, 164-166

Tchernichovsky, Shaul – 29, 60

The Twelfth Planet – 10, 13, 31, 37, 74, 79, 100, 128, 136, 141, 151-154, 156, 166

Tiamat – 4-7, 10-12, 15, 18-38, 40, 41, 44-51, 53, 55, 56, 60, 60, 69, 70, 73, 133, 134

Ti-it (tit) – 61, 134

Ubartutu – 78

Uranus – 7, 9, 10, 19, 21, 37, 45, 47, 49, 73

Utu – 7, 68, 69, 71, 74, 89, 160

Voyager 1, 2 – 39

Yahweh – 3, 5, 7, 59, 61, 77, 78, 84, 87, 88, 92, 95, 96, 98, 99, 104, 105, 110, 118-125, 130, 135, 137, 140-143, 146, 149, 150, 155, 160, 162, 164, 165

www.ingramcontent.com/pod-product-compliance
Lightning Source LLC
Chambersburg PA
CBHW041621220426
43662CB00001B/1